CONNIE KERBS

PATHS
OF
FEAR

An Anthology of Overcoming Through
Courage, Inspiration, and Love

**Forthcoming Titles
in the
Pebbled Lane Books Series**
(F.I.N.E. Reads Press)

Paths of Courage
Paths of Friendship
Paths of Gratitude
Paths of Renewal
With more titles to come

PATHS OF FEAR

An Anthology of Overcoming Through
Courage, Inspiration, and Love

By
Connie Kerbs
Pebbled Lane Books
Published by
F.I.N.E. Reads Press

www.finereadspress.com
www.pebbledlanebooks.com

Copyright © 2016
By Connie Kerbs

All rights reserved. This book or any portion thereof may not be reproduced or used in any manner whatsoever without the express written permission of the author, publisher, or their authorized representatives, except for the use of brief quotations embodied in articles and reviews.

All quotations remain the intellectual property of their respective originators. All use of quotations has been done with permission or under the fair use copyright principle.

Printed in the United States of America

ISBN: 978-0996966115

Library of Congress Control Number: 2016900921

BISAC: SEL021000 SELF-HELP/Motivational & Inspirational

Pebbled Lane Books
An imprint of
F.I.N.E. Reads Press
Clayton, WA
www.finereadspress.com
www.pebbledlanebooks.com
www.conniekerbs.com

Please email any inquiries to the author at:
connie.kerbs@aol.com
or the publisher at
info@finereadspress.com

Dedication

To my elementary orchestra buddy and high school sweetheart, my best friend, my beloved eternal companion – my mate of all these years; it is to you I dedicate this book: Thank you forever, just for being you, and loving me for me. There aren't enough stars in all the heavens by which to measure my admiration of you or this amazing life and love we have been blessed to live. Truly, this book, and my life's dream of writing wouldn't have been realized anytime soon without your love and support.

I also dedicate these pages to *All* the children in my world who have made me *mother*: natural, adopted, fostered, and angel-winged. There aren't enough petals on all the flowers in all the world to count the ways you have blessed me. There aren't enough grains of sand in all the oceans to measure my individual love and gratitude for you.

My dedication would be grossly incomplete without mentioning He who hath buoyed me up, lifted me up, and filled me up, without and within. He hath overflowed my cup with grace and gratitude, until there was no room for doubt or fear in my heart. Indeed:

Could we with ink the ocean fill,
And were the heavens of parchment made,
Were every stalk on earth a quill,
And every man a scribe by trade;
To write the love of God above,
Would drain the ocean dry;
Nor could the scroll contain the whole,
Though stretched from sky to sky

Meir Ben Isaac Nehorai

Acknowledgements

With special thanks, I want to acknowledge Michelle Tupy, (www.michelletupy.com), writer, editor, blog-writer, muse-cheerleader, devoted wife, inspiring mom, philanthropist and a world-traveling homeschooler. My friend.

Without her encouragement and professional support, Paths of Fear would likely have never had all it would need to overcome itself -at least not anytime soon.

Gratitude is not only the greatest of virtues, but the parent of all the others.
Marcus Tullius Cicero

Disclaimer

This book is designed to provide quality entertainment, enlightenment, and encouragement to our readers. It is sold with the understanding that the publisher and its contributing authors are not rendering any physical, mental, emotional, psychological, legal, or any other kind of professional advice. The content of each article is the sole expression and opinion of its particular author, and not necessarily that of the publisher, or book's principal author. No warranties or guarantees are expressed or implied by the author/editor/publisher's choice to include any of the content in this volume. Neither the publisher nor the individual editor(s)/author(s) shall be liable for any physical, psychological, emotional, financial, or commercial damages, including, but not limited to, special, incidental, consequential or other damages. As we are also, readers are responsible for their own choices, actions, and results.

Further, no part or portion of this book may be copied, reproduced, electronically shared or stored without the publisher's, author's or individual contributor's express permission to do so, except in the case of media/literary reviews.

Several names and identifying details have been changed to protect individual and circumstantial privacy.

Courage is fear that has said its prayers.
Dorothy Bernard

Table of Contents

Dedication..v

Acknowledgements..vii

Disclaimer..ix

Foreword..xvii
    By Alex Couley

Introduction..xxiii
    By Connie Kerbs

Poetic Pause..xxxiii

Ambition..xxiii
    By Samantha Brown

Chapter 1

Stories...1

    Square Dance..3
        By Cindy Matthews

    Malignant...9
        By Karen Peebles

    Dreaming Dreams and Facing Fears 13
        By Robert B. Robeson

    The Flood..23
        By Nicole Pinkman

    Perfect...29
        By Christina Hamlett

    The Carnival Ride 33
        By Connie Kerbs

    Choice Not Circumstance 39
        By Tina Jensen

    Iron Ana..43
        By Ana Hernández Millán

Brush it off Darlin' 47
   By Mary Law Meinelt

Fear Coach 55
   By Niall McInnes

Poetic Pause 59

Life: From Three Best Things…. (Work, Love, and Life) ... 61
   By Henry Van Dyke (1852-1933)

CHAPTER 2

The Hands That Rock The Cradle 63

Honey, I Killed Our Kid 65
   By Cory Bartlett

What is Fear? 71
   By Lainie Liberti

Poetic Pause 77

The Sick Child 79
   By: Robert Louis Stevenson

CHAPTER 3

Speaking Of 81

Clarity 83
   By Jonty Bush

The Fear Phenomenon 85
   By Roxanie Lebsanft

Poetic Pause 89

Fear in Facets 91
   By Cesar Moran-Cahusac

CHAPTER 4

Nuts and Bolts 93

- Fight, Flight or Freeze 95
  By Connie Kerbs

- Dying to Fly 103
  By Ray Wood

- Fears and Phobias Galore 107
  By Samantha Raes

- Poetic Pause 113

- Fear, a Monster 115
  By Cesar Moran-Cahusac

CHAPTER 5

A Literary Legacy 117

- The Boneyard Boys 119
  By Connie Kerbs

- A Night-Piece on Death 125
  By Thomas Parnell

- Fate's Irony 131
  An Ancient Talmud Text Unknown Author

- Poetic Pause 133

- A Rebuttal to the Boneyard Boys 135
  By Henry Lawson (1892)

CHAPTER 6

From The Mouths Of Babes 137

- The Transfusion 139
  Unknown

Fear of… 141
   By Emilia Tupy

Poetic Pause 143

If- 145
   By Rudyard Kipling

CHAPTER 7

Mustard Seeds 149

Supplications 151
   By Connie Kerbs

Godly Fear 157
   By Connie Kerbs

Fear Not 163
   By Connie Kerbs

Bible Verses On Fear 171
   By Connie Kerbs

Poetic Pause 173

Abide With Me 175
   By Henry Francis Lyte

CHAPTER 8

The Best Medicine 177

Mortality Rates 179
   By Nancy Raymond

Poetic Pause 183

Scaredy-Cat 185
   By Connie Kerbs

Chapter 9

In Summary 187

Conclusions 189
By Connie Kerbs

Poetic Pause 193

The Elderly Gentleman 195
By George Canning)

Chapter 10

For The Love Of Quotes 197

Pebbles To Pocket: Overcoming Fear 199
A Collection of Novice Voices & Sages of the Ages

Poetic Pause 203

Epitaph 205
Samuel Taylor Coleridge

Chapter 11

Precious Pearls 209

"The Love of God." 211
Meir Ben Isaac Nehorai's (The Akdumut, circa 1050)

Seasons 215
Anonymous, from Ecclesiastes (KJV)

Beauty for Ashes 217
The Prophet Isaiah (KJV)

Amazing Grace 219
By John Newton (1725-1807)

In Flanders Fields 223
By Lieutenant-Colonel John McCrae

Nothing Gold Can Stay 227
    By Robert Lee Frost

More Inspirational Pebbles:On Anything & Everything....229
    Gathered by Connie Kerbs

Poetic Pause 233

Love and Fear 235
    By G.W. Mercure

CHAPTER 12

Pondering Poetry 237

To Lord Byron 238
    By John Keats

Some Prosy on Poesy 239
    By Connie Kerbs

More Pebbles On Poetry 241
    Collected by Connie Kerbs

Poetic Pause 243

Poetry's Space: Part 1 From Poetry's Palace 243
    Connie Kerbs

CHAPTER 13

The Beginning Of The End 247

Word 249
    Martin Luther

An Intercession 251
    By Paul, the Apostle

Bibliography 253

About the Author 257
    Connie Kerbs

About Pebbled Lane Books 258

Foreword

By Alex Couley

Here it is my intention to share my thoughts with you in two parts. The first part is why I recommend to you this valuable literary body of work, and part two will be my specific thoughts on the subject at hand, which is fear itself.

I recently attended a conference at one of the world's leading universities. One of the keynote speakers quoted Eleanor Roosevelt. The quote: "Do one thing every day that scares you." As a whole, the audience loved this quote and received enthusiastically the sentiments that lay behind it. I, however, was left feeling a little perplexed. I had to ask myself whether I wanted to wake up every day trying to think of something that scares me, and then tackle it. Is that leading a positive, fulfilled life?

I suggest that we have lost our way in our interaction with our emotions. It is not about how to eradicate or challenge our emotional nature. Our pathway is more about accepting that we are feeling entities who have learned how to think. Our deep emotional experiences are at the very core of our being. Put simply, we are what we feel. A healthy part of our journey is accepting that we all interact with these emotional experiences in different ways. As a person at different developmental and experiential stages of our lives, we will even individually respond in unique and various ways. In other words, even our maturing selves will think, see, and feel differently than the younger, less experienced version of us.

When we seek inspiration, it is easy to look at examples that might represent world-changing events. But we can't all be Rosa Parks; we can't all stand in front of a tank in Tiananmen Square.

When I look for inspiration, I want to be able to relate the message to one I can translate to my life.

This collection addresses the above two points. Here, people tell of their unique interaction with this emotion we call fear. They represent a wide range and diversity within our community. I hope it gives you encouragement when you need it, and in ways you need it.

Science widely accepts that all humans have two innate fears: the fear of falling and fear of loud noises. The consensus is that all other fears are acquired. It's helpful to appreciate the role science tells us fear has likely played throughout human history and development. People now refer to the well-known Fight-or-Flight response system.

However, that is not quite a complete picture. When we are very afraid, neither fight nor flight is possible. At that point, we freeze. For this reason, a more authentic representation of the process is Fight, Flight or Freeze.

Modern technology now affords us to see what is happening in the brain when this process kicks in. When our sensory organs recognize or perceive a threat, they fire a message to a part of the brain known as the amygdala. The amygdala then stimulates the body with stress hormones. Long-term and frequent exposure to these hormones is extremely detrimental to our overall health. All the more reason to consider Eleanor Roosevelt's advice more figuratively, than literally.

That being said, in the practical field of psychology, treating fear is often based on the idea of exposing someone to their fears in a safe, structured, manner. This gradual technique increases the fear stimulus over time, which gently rewrites the fear message. It can do a kind of reprogramming of the brain to understand there is no basis for the fear; it shuts off the false alarm.

Another way psychology attempts to put practical application to work by helping people face fears is almost the exact opposite. In a controversial process known as "flooding," the person is immersed fully into their fear in a major exposure. An example would be taking someone who is afraid of dogs, and leaving them in a kennel with numerous large canines.

Both approaches result in degrees of success and failure. This mixed outcome should be considered thoughtfully, with individual capacities in mind, as well as other environmental circumstances that would influence the potential for success and the risks involved.

Putting this together means that, while many of the wrong kinds of frequent exposure to fear can become physiologically and otherwise psychologically unhealthy, concerted confrontations to stifling fear can be helpful. The reason being, fear itself is mainly a learned response. Therefore, it is reasonable to propose that if it is learned it can be unlearned. This idea, of course, is not a one size fits all solution to perceived problems with fear. It does give options and hope, however, for folks dealing with phobias they need to overcome, such as an executive whose fear of flying is interfering with his career.

Fear's powerful effects upon us are just a piece of the puzzle. Here is another aspect: it is just a simple, but the essential question to ask. Filtering our phobias through this idea, as well as larger issues of fear in life may be extremely helpful. We should ask, "Will facing the fear improve someone else's life?" Here is why I propose this somewhat undersold, but extremely helpful postulate. It's very simple.

We are a tribal species; a complex organism hard-wired to cooperate with one another. Our intrinsic commitment to others is a powerful motivator, as well as a dynamic force weaved throughout our life. We naturally go the extra mile to help others, especially those we care for. Ever heard of, "mother bear syndrome?"

It is not news to anyone that attentive parents will make an extra effort for their children, unquestioningly, including sacrifice they wouldn't make for themselves. This tendency is in the hardwiring of our species, embedded deeply in the DNA even, and it isn't exclusive to the parent-child relationship, even if that is one of the most obvious representations of it. I would propose to you, sometimes simply asking who else will benefit can be enough to give you the courage and focus on moving forward.

In conclusion, at some point in our lives, we will likely all face fear. Beyond the initial knee-jerk response known as Flight.

Flight or Freeze, we are confronted with the decision about what we do next in response to whatever challenge we face. These difficult experiences may have a strong perceived fear label attached. It's good to remember we have many thoughtful options to choose from.

We can face the fear head-on, with total immersion, or "flooding." We can gradually face the fear, with controlled exposure, in small bites we feel we can chew. We can work with powerful built-in motivators which kick us into gear. But, is that it?

There is another option, often missed, but which may be helpful: avoidance. Yes. That's right. Avoid it. Until another time, if that should ever come, when we are more motivated to overcome it or when life's demands truly call for it. We can set it aside until the energy, focus, and patience required to tackle the problem are in optimum balance. Sometimes this is the wisest choice, regardless of social pressures to *always* facing our fears.

I suggest to you now that these are all legitimate, solutions. However, only you can decide which way is right, and the timing of such scenarios. Ask yourself, "Do I have the strength at this point, to make worthwhile progress on this issue?" Then, "What exactly will I gain from expending the energy to address this fear?" Clarifying our purpose or motives to achieve something is a valid, healthy fear response.

In this way, we can utilize a thoughtful decision-making process that weighs multiple factors and higher orders of thinking such as the altruistic, tribal-oriented ones already mentioned. Otherwise, we might be operating on impulse, or uncontrollable reactions to a perceived threat, or perhaps the hype of popular messages that don't individually apply to us at the time. This key problem-solving time enables humans to achieve optimum survival, as well as the greatest potential for our thriving as thinking, complex, social beings.

Practice consciously, in the Freeze opportunity of fear, the simple question:

Will facing this fear improve anyone else's life?

This singular self-query broadens your vantage point offering clarity and a deeper sense of control in life.

As a final thought, I would encourage everyone to remember, life is about being the best version of you, and just because someone else says you should do this or that or be *fearless* about this or that, doesn't necessarily make it true.

Sincerely,
Alex Couley
International Centre for Leadership Coaching
http://iclc.com.au/

Alex Couley is an international figure in mental health, coaching, and positive psychology. He is a Founding Fellow of the Institute of Coaching at Harvard University, an affiliate of the Institute's Coaching leadership forum and also sits on the Harvard Business Review's advisory panel on coaching. Alex's background is as a clinician in the mental health field for 37 years. He is an author and regular conference presenter on mental health issues, coaching, and positive psychology interventions. (Alex at alex.couley@hushmail.com.)

Remember, the tallest oak was once just a little nut that held its ground.

Unknown

Introduction

By Connie Kerbs

I am simply in awe of this project. I am also thrilled with the ways it has defined itself. Ultimately, this anthology on fear, like the entire Pebbled Lane Books Series it is part of, has become a compelling mission. Each of the pieces here emerged, filtered humbly out of many powerful writings; each submitted honestly, vulnerable, courageously. Each echoes the essence of this emotional theme in unique, universal, and practical forms.

Every essay, poem, and story consists of prevailing events, lives, and people who experienced life-changing fears of one kind or another. I find their willingness to share these vulnerable exposures for the possibility of lighting someone else's path, both inspiring and admirable.

The Real Story

To be sure, *Paths of Fear* could have just as well been *Paths of Courage* or *Paths of Hope,* or for that matter *Paths of Love*. It is, after all, not *only* about the suffering or darkness which fearful circumstances invoke. While these serve as a necessary backdrop, they are a means to an end to illustrate the essential story which transcends the details. These powerful narrations of fear also show how others have endured and overcome their trials. These display a brightness of hope, an unstoppable, swelling of human dignity, and a full embracing of life, in all its robust imperfection.

To my delight, this work has unexpectedly taken the shape of a surprise, ultimate theme; one we might not readily connect with *fear.* This underlying thesis has a subtle supposition here: that there is only one over-arching, undeniable solution to all our fears. The answer to fear, in the end it seems, is just love, in all its imperfection, depth and contours.

Alex Couley, in the foreword, coined it remarkably:

We are a tribal species; a complex organism hard-wired to co-operate with one another. Our intrinsic care and genuine commitment to others are powerful motivators. They make for compelling experiences that define us and outline our life.

Most of the narratives in this book on fear speak to one form of love or another, directly or otherwise. This riveting emotional catalyst can be for our parent, child, self, our higher power, pet, spouse – even patriotism. In the end, our overcoming often boils down to the love we have for *something* or *someone* which sees us through. It is also a slice of just how that commitment, and our stick-with-it-ness to it, turns out for us.

Without committed love, its motivation and success, it's striving, its absence or withdrawal, the sting of betrayal, misguided use - or twisted abuse, there is no risk. With no risk, there is little to fear, therefore, no story, at least not for this book.

The Collection

This compelling display of the human heart shows some of the many ways we cope with acute, fear-based emotional duress. We are also privy here to lives marked with poignant long-suffering - sometimes endured for unthinkable chunks of time.

Other narratives offer absorbing excursions down winding *paths of fear*, though some more cringe-worthy than others.

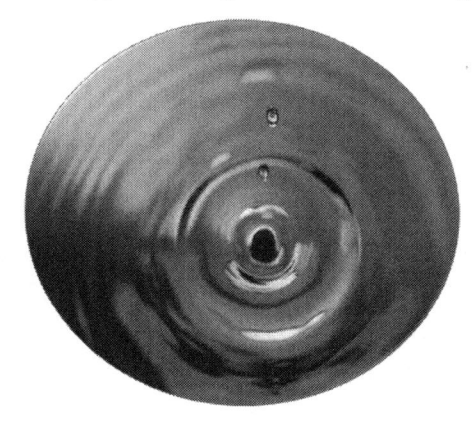

Others distill the less individual and more everyday anxieties which imbue many of our hopes and desires. These passages outline our more universal experiences.

Like a pebble rippling placid water, some of the stories here show how the *little things* in life – are anything but. We can see how seemingly insignificant details provoke paradigm shifts like cataclysmic events.

These remind us of the juiciness of life, and how paramount the everyday journey is in overcoming our challenges and experiencing a fullness of joy.

Of course, what good would such a collection be which displays such a sampling of the human struggle without proposing at least some viable answers to these struggles of the ages? Bold, refreshing ideas infused with timeless wisdom are the meat of this project. These nurture our visions of success and encourage our best version of ourselves to emerge and thrive.

Focusing a spiritual lens offers a deeper understanding of this primal mechanism called fear, and its over-arching influence upon us. Like a magnifying glass, healthy, positive, spiritual connections offer clarity to otherwise fuzzy solutions. Like a compass, these afford subtle course corrections that influence our trajectory. They drastically affect not only our daily experience and quality of life but are often all-important to long-range outcomes.

Being as happy and effective of a person we can through everything life will bring, including our ages and stages, health and wealth, (or lack thereof), does not just happen for most of us. It takes continued compassing, work (course correction) on our attitude and perspective.

Diligence in this area has huge dividends over time that cannot be underestimated or substituted. Several passages and poems, if not most of them laced thoughout throughout this project illustrate this.

A few of the stories here won't even apologize for haunting unsuspecting readers. These stark memoirs will etch an indelible mark, inviting a reluctant, permanent notation on a reader's soul about some of humanity's undeniable suffering and ugliness.

At the same time, they provide an enduring testament to the feistiest courage and that innate experience we call human dignity: a thing which in the end, will rarely be denied.

Some stories here show some of the best living, breathing examples of acceptance, grace, and overcoming humanly possible. Whether such endurances have already been well-captured, and prominently retold, others have been more obscure until being reincarnated for something like this anthology. All are shining examples of overcoming in inspiring, ways.

In addition to the main *Stories* section, you can meander through other clusters of essays, articles, and works, such as *Speaking Of,* which present interesting nuances to the *fear* theme. These offer a unique perspective to the bulk of memoirs that make up *Paths of Fear*: a different *take* if you will.

In *The Hands that Rock the Cradle*, you'll uncover representations that illustrate real parental fear, sometimes called *Momma Bear Syn-*

drome. This misleading moniker represents a universal parental concept, as even fathers of human offspring are far from spared. It is a special compote of emotions layered with fear that is rooted in the basal, instinctive need to protect our young: a primal fear.

Indeed, woven into our DNA, fear is an ingenious tool. Essentially innate, it is a highly sensitive, and effective warning system. Fear properly employed, exponentially improves our odds of individual and species survival. It can also bring vital Intel to any of our many complex psycho-social balancing acts.

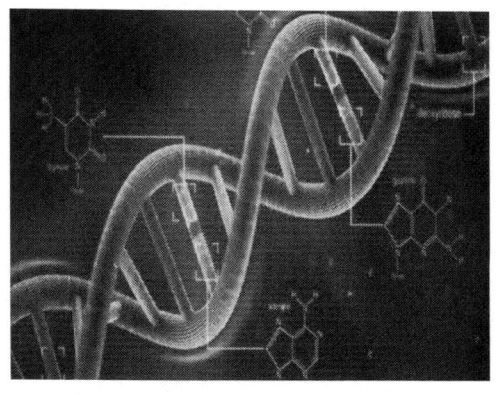

The *Mustard Seeds* section clusters the spiritually inclined passages together. Paths of Fear seeks to be an authentic, inspirational work, but generic enough to be accessible to a wide swath of perspectives. Fear, after all, is not a copyrighted emotion, nor is it particularly immune or attached to any race, religion or income bracket. Rather, fear is a most human sensation, a crucial emotion that reminds us we are more the same than different.

I have felt from its inception this series and the individual works within have a *joyful burden* to propose something worthwhile about faith and its role in the various themes explored throughout. Sincere religious sentiments certainly have advisements for us on something as deeply important and reoccurring as fear in our life.

Without exception, *ALL* religious structures put significant stock into fear's greatest catalyst *AND* magnifier – love. Let me repeat that. Fear's greatest catalyst and magnifier is love. What? How?

I proposed earlier, that to my surprise, fear's greatest solution has revealed itself in these very pages to be….love. Of course, each story is a clear demonstration of love's lack or (potential) loss or misuse being the root of trouble. Hence, love is both the cause and the solution to most of our deepest troubles; a true paradox.

This contradiction seems to be one of the greatest, most misunderstood ironies of the human condition. The very same category of emotional experiences which lay us to waste from time to time – has the unequivocal power to replace fear in our life with exquisite joy. The very substance of Pandora's Box of misery, and ultimately our greatest Achilles' Heel – is also the ultimate fear- neutralizer, clarifier, antithesis, an authentic cure-all, and the unintended, but gloriously emerged theme of this book— love.

But how can this be? How can love impact us in such extremely different ways – some negative and some positive.

This very question is what EVERY meaningful, substantive religious form has grappled with throughout the ages. In fact, it is arguable that all functional spiritually oriented constructs make qualitative attempts at understanding this compelling problem called love – and harnessing this universal remedy to most of our problems: love in one form or another, that is.

Love is, after all, a reckoning force, a most interesting and complicated, emotional, spiritual, even physical element woven throughout our life experiences. This aspect of the human condition seems to be inescapable, whether it be the pleasing effects of the presence of love in our life – or the most intensely poignant experience of its premature, abnormal or unexpected absence.

This thing called love (or *charity* in certain circles) also comes in countless forms: love of family, parent, child, mate, friend, pet or even self. In the case of religion, the primary focus is the devotion towards a devout and sincere concept of a Divine Creator or God, and or such supernatural being's extensions or representatives. It is a given for those with religious tendencies, that this omniscient power or being takes a caring, encouraging role in our lives.

The truth is if there were a way to write a book with any breadth and depth on the circus called fear, and its only authentic ringmaster called love – without including the crowd-pleasing menagerie that is religion – I don't know of any.

And so, like the Pebbled Lane Books series it is part of, Paths of Fear, is in the end, woven together with an accessible combination of core Judeo-Christian values, all the while acknowledging the undeniable spirituality hinted at through universal, *wisdom of the ages*.

As its name would suggest, the chapter, *Mustard Seeds*, springboards from such a religious premise. This section, also a hallmark of the Pebbled Lane Books series, explores the book's theme through the accepted canons of this long-standing religious legacy: the Old and New Testaments. The heartfelt essays planted in this section hope to cause a gentle stir in the heart of any soul willing to entertain a storehouse of metaphors and ancient textual (biblical) examples of life's challenges, societal problems, and some of that which we must come to terms within our deepest selves – our soul.

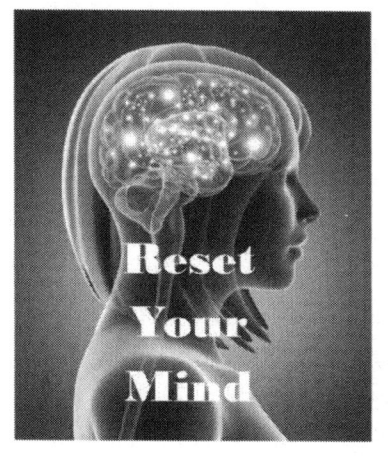

In between all the sections, I have placed *A Poetic Pause*, which is just that. This self-explanatory instant lets readers take a breath, and invites the heart and brain to reboot for a moment. I have bought, hook line and sinker, into the proposal that poetry stimulates our neurophysiology where music and rhythm all connect with math and language. In other words, this infuses our rational selves with a fresh shot of creative juices! This can give our *problem solver* an amazing, natural, and energizing boost! Never underestimate the power of poetry!

Explore both universal and niche fear experiences in the Nuts and Bolts Chapter. Passages here round out the narratives and poetry with pertinent, helpful information. Learning how others have coped with their fears encourages a potent antidote to the toxic, unwanted side effects of overwhelming fear which tries to rear its ugly head in our inner-world from time to time. Further, learning how others have been protected, changed, and ultimately motivated by fear's relentless stirring—inspires us.

Paths of Fear hopes to contribute a unique, empowering take on the collective experience called *fear*. Its ultimate purpose is to offer a quality drop in the bucket of efficacy to deal with the many, fear-inducing curveballs of life, which we all encounter eventually.

And so I submit to you, dearest readers, Paths of Fear, because:

Our deepest fear is not that we are inadequate. Our deepest fear is that we are powerful beyond measure. It is our light, not our darkness that most frightens us. We ask ourselves, "Who am I to be brilliant, gorgeous, talented, and fabulous?" Actually, who are you not to be? You are a child of God. Your playing small does not serve the world. There is nothing enlightened about shrinking so that other people will not feel insecure around you. We are all meant to shine, as children do. We were born to make manifest the glory of God that is within us. It is not just in some of us; it is in everyone, and as we let our own light shine, we unconsciously give others permission to do the same...(2)

Printed With Permission From Marianne Williams'
A Return To Love.
(Note: this passage is often wrongly credited to Nelson Mandela.)

People everywhere are the same;
they are all people to be loved.
They are all hungry for love.

Mother Teresa

Poetic Pause

Poetry Pebbles

Poetry lifts the veil from the hidden beauty of the world and makes familiar objects be as if they were not familiar.

Percy Bysshe Shelley

Poetry is the spontaneous overflow of powerful feelings: it takes its origin from emotion recollected in tranquility.

William Wordsworth

Ambition

By Samantha Brown

A narrow path, to slip… is to fall.
Presume… I shall not, will not, could not?
Absurd! But for grace, I shall crawl.
Solemn hours, endless days,
Looming bleak eternal round.
Reward…To know who I truly am
Through falling, I have found.

Samantha Brown lives with her husband and children in an exceptionally beautiful area of the Inland Northwest, with a mountain of her own to call home. She enjoys the wildlife, her bees, the occasional owlet, showing Shabby Chic how it's done, and, being all around uber-artistic and crafty. When she is not playing with clay, playing with her children, or playing with her menagerie of furry friends—she is probably out riding her bike or working on that marathon goal with her new and improved "bionic" leg.

Never fear trying something new. Remember, amateurs built the ark; professionals built the Titanic.

Unknown

Chapter 1

Stories

Inspired

When a resolute young fellow steps up to the great bully, the world, and takes him boldly by the beard, he is often surprised to find it comes off in his hand, and that it was only tied on to scare away the timid adventurers.

Ralph Waldo Emerson

Misfortune had made Lily supple instead of hardening her, and a pliable substance is less easy to break than a stiff one.

Edith Wharton, The House of Mirth (1905)

I learned from the example of my father that the manner in which one endures what must be endured is more important than the thing that must be endured.

Francis Bacon

Be not afraid of life. Believe that life is worth living, and your belief will help create the fact.

William James (1897)

Well, we all make mistakes, dear, so just put it behind you. We should regret our mistakes and learn from them, but never carry them forward into the future with us.

L.M. Montgomery

Square Dance

By Cindy Matthews

Wayne stood to my left. When the music began, he nestled my fingers in his mitten-sized hands before steering me toward three other couples, our shoulders scarcely touching. I couldn't make sense of the complexity of the required steps. My jaw finally unclenched when the teacher lifted the needle from the record.

"Relax your shoulders. You're awfully uptight." Wayne's voice was liquid honey in my ears. When he smiled, a gold tooth glistened.

I had a right to be bad-tempered. Square dancing with Wayne was draining. He was, after all, a grade twelve student and I was only in grade nine. Our two gym classes had collided for a five-day unit on traditional forms of dance.

Before the next song, Wayne pushed long fingers through his thick auburn hair. He looked older than other grade-twelve guys. He wore cologne, something musky. Whiskers bristled along his jawline. He was so hip with his colorful striped shirt and faded jean jacket. Wayne was our school's drug dealer.

"You aren't nervous to be around me, are you?" he asked.

Wayne was an imposing figure next to my petite build. I opened and closed my mouth before lifting stringy blond hair off my moist brow. I adjusted my T-shirt and looked away from Wayne, willing myself to relax by gulping deep breaths. Before the teacher finished instructing us on the finer points of the promenade, Wayne reached again for my limp, sticky fingers.

"Ah, look at that. You've got a boyfriend." Wayne patted the ring on my left hand.

"Excuse me. I don't feel so good." I rushed from the gymnasium and headed for the girls' bathroom.

After last class, I boarded my yellow school bus headed for home. All the good seats near the back overflowed with occupants, so I dumped my backpack on a seat near the driver. He flicked the defroster on high, filling the front of the bus with a blast of heat and buzzing noise. As the driver pulled out of the parking lot, I took in the snowy scene up ahead. Late afternoon January sunlight flickered on my jeans. We passed the faceless, boarded remains of an abandoned castle. Crushed corn stalks stood at attention in the snow-covered fields. I could hardly wait to get home and tell my mother about Wayne.

Our home rested on eleven acres a few miles from the high school. The driveway was three hundred yards long and often became drifted in with snow. Today was no different than most winter days. I stepped off the bus into a mound of snow.

"Take care," the driver said before closing the collapsible door against the fierce wind.

I tied my hood under my chin. The temperature felt much colder than when I had boarded the bus in the morning. Snowflakes fastened like burrs to the hairs dotting my face.

"Come on," I groaned when I remembered I'd left my mittens in my locker. "This day can't get any worse."

I folded my fingers into the sleeves of my parka before clutching my backpack against my chest. I used the heels of my boots to punch into the two-foot drifts. Snow draping nearby branches made the trees look magical. Our bungalow, off in the distance, seemed to pitch and sway in the wind before disappearing in swirls of snow.

The smell hit me first. Diesel. Then the insistent purr of an engine. I glanced over my shoulder and spotted a tractor, a stream of snow bursting from its large blower; it was the farmer we hired to blow out our driveway.

"Why now? The storm's just started." My words eddied in the wind.

The farmer gestured at me to climb aboard. As we inched toward the bungalow, I noticed my father standing in the doorway to the house. His hand held the screen door open a few inches. His face appeared drawn, and the space between his eyebrows furrowed. Despite the coldness of the day, my body felt clammy. Once the farmer had pulled up close enough, I stepped down from the tractor and ran for the house.

My father tugged me inside. "It's your mother."

The smell of vomit and filled my nose. And maybe feces. My father shook his head before turning away wiping a cheek. "I was busy with the chickens, and when I finally came in, I found her slumped on the floor."

He pulled me against his chest and squeezed. The smell of stale coffee was on his breath. I could feel that his shirt was damp. The noise of sirens pierced the air as my father's heart pounded, my arms dangling beside my legs like cinder blocks.

A beige ambulance pulled up to the house, its beacons flashing. The attendants dragged a stretcher into the house. One of them patted my father on the shoulder. "Where is the patient?"

"I'll show you." My father's voice was low and gravelly.

I couldn't recall when I'd set my school bag on the desk by the door. It towered over two empty, plastic pill containers. Pink pills for sleeping and white ones for anxiety. I placed a hand on my chest and noticed how my body recoiled with the nerves of a coward. I pivoted toward the couch and prepared myself for bad news. The attendants were in the next room. They spoke in short sentences in a manner that sounded more like dogs barking than anything. My father hovered in the doorway to the bedroom, folding and unfolding his hands like he wasn't sure of the protocol. His eyes had locked on mine before he mouthed, "What if--?"

What bound me to him in that instant was a shared belief that death could be imminent. We had faced this sort of predicament before. When I was seven, she was diagnosed with cervical cancer. I just coiled up in my bed every day after school until she got better.

Grappling with the implausible is overwhelming for an underdeveloped brain.

A year later, Mother quit medications prescribed for a nervous condition. The pills kept her balanced. Without them, her behavior turned erratic. During one episode, she got picked up by police for threatening customers at K-Mart and had to be wrestled into a straight jacket.

Only two others in my whole school had parents who had died, and those students were messed-up. I didn't want to be them. I interlaced my fingers, feigning prayer. That's what people who aren't religious do.

There were things I would miss if she were to die. Who would pick me up from gymnastics? Who would listen to me complain about square dancing and Wayne? What would I do when mid-terms came, and I freaked out about Shakespeare? Who would ever be there to make me potato pancakes?

By the time emergency personnel strapped her to the stretcher, we had headed to the car. I fumbled with the just grabbed empty pill containers now riding deep in my pocket. I slipped into the passenger seat and tugged the belt tight across my chest. Dad and I exchanged small talk as we followed the beacon lights to the hospital.

As I watched the wipers pass over the snow-streaked windshield, I wished I understood why my mother liked to hurt us. When my father finished parking the car, I bolted for the emergency department. His voice called, "Be careful. Wait for me." But I didn't want to delay a moment longer. With nimble legs, I raced for the brightly-lit institution. The foyer and nearby waiting area felt spotless and weightless with light. Someone coughing bent over or complaining occupied every seat.

Mother's stretcher evaporated from view. My father moved past me and plunked with concern on a chair opposite the triage nurse. He spoke like an agitated cartoon character, his hands waving in the air until the nurse granted him the right to go behind the turquoise screen where my mother was. I remained where I was, too apprehensive to leave the security the waiting room offered. Eventually, a mother and her two children waddled off, so I claimed their chairs. The people around me seemed to whisper-talk, but I had no notion to share their worries. I stretched across two armless chairs and fell into a restless sleep. By the time my father returned, it was light out.

"Your mother made it."

Your mother. Not Resi or Resl or even Mom. Your mother. I kicked the chair leg with the heel of my boot. My body was on fire like someone had touched my skin with the end of a lit cigarette. I felt wrung out as I'd just come out the other side with a high fever. I felt flat, too, like I'd made a stellar play on the volleyball court, yet no one noticed.

"Did you speak to her?" I asked.

"Yes," I spoke. Her throat is raw. From charcoal the doctors had to pump into her."

I gave him a withering look.

"She'll have to stay here a while. Maybe go to London Psych. She's very ill, you know."

I sighed. "Did you ask her why?"

My father's eyes narrowed. Nothing prepares you for some things.

"I don't know how much more of this I can take," he said.

I turned from him and ran. I followed King Street to Green to Victoria. I fled, fully awake now. I jogged along the sidewalk until I reached a park. I kicked snow from a bench and stiffly sat until I stopped feeling cold. I twisted the tight, metal band on my finger until it came loose. A gift from my father. Not from my boyfriend, like Wayne had said. I chucked the ring far into the snow.

"It was too snug, anyway," I said, before standing to cross the street and make my way back.

Cindy Matthews writes, paints, and instructs online courses for teachers in Ontario, Canada. Her fiction and nonfiction have appeared in Canada, USA, UK, South Africa, and Australia. 'Clutched by the Hair' was awarded Top 3 in the 2015 Desi Writers' Lounge Fiction Writing Contest. 'Ringo,' a creative nonfiction piece, was awarded third prize at the 2015 Northwestern Ontario Writers Workshop Writing Contest. 'Nothing by Mouth' was shortlisted in the 2014 Event Magazine Non-Fiction Contest and was recently published by Tincture, Australia. Find her at www.facebook/CindyIsabel Matthews or @Matthec1957.

May you LIVE every day of your life!
Jonathan Swift

Malignant

By Karen Peebles

When I was 30, I married the man of my dreams. He was loving and gentle, everything I had hoped for and more. The following year we had a beautiful baby daughter, then a son two years after. Life was joyful in those early years while we built our marriage and our family.

After the birth of our son, my husband's behavior started to change. John became increasingly irritated by my company and started verbally abusing me. This hostility grew in time, to the point where his irritation with me was constant, and finally replaced with hatred and contempt. The dramatic change in John's personality left me with a complete loss of understanding what had happened to us.

After two years of dealing with the daily anger and hatred that my husband felt toward me, I took advantage of a moment when we were both sitting at the breakfast table drinking coffee. I told John that I wanted a divorce, and I asked him if we could talk about the details of how we would continue to parent our children separately.

John excused himself from the table. "Hold on; I'll be right back," he said. "Sit tight." In less than a minute, I heard the metal click of a handgun hammer pulled back. It was less than an inch from my right ear. As the courage drained out of my body I heard John's voice in the other ear, "Don't ever say the word 'divorce' to me again, or I'll blow your head off. Do you understand me?" he asked. I nodded my head quickly as hot tears slipped from my eyes.

Over the next couple of years, I tried to find a way out of the marriage. Many times, I had packed a small bag of clothes for the kids and me and had hidden it in the bottom of my closet, waiting for the chance to slip out when the time was right. On one of these occasions,

I was one day away from leaving with the children and moving to a place where he would not be able to find us. We were only one day from that beautiful freedom when he found our little suitcase.

This time, when the gun came out, I was sure it was the end. I could smell the metal as he shoved the end of the barrel into my face. The hammer clicked back. I closed my eyes and thought about our children being raised by this lunatic. I held my breath. My life paraded in front of my closed eyes. John spoke. "You can't go far enough," he said. "There is no place where I will not find you. No matter how long it takes me, I will find you. And when I do, it'll be a bloody mess."

I looked at John. "Don't ever get sick," I said to him. "You can make me stay, but be careful that you don't get sick because I will not take care of you." He laughed long and hard and pulled the gun back away from my face. "Don't worry," he answered. "I'm young and healthy," he laughed again. How that laugh made my skin crawl.

From that day, I counted the years until the kids would be grown, and I would leave John. I would not risk their lives, but once they left, I would risk mine. Even death would have been better than remaining in that marriage. It would be twelve years until I could leave. Our son would turn 18 in that time, and leave home. I convinced myself that was not so long of time. I would manage it, somehow.

During the day, while John was at work, I homeschooled the children and raised them in the same way that any other mother would. Our days brimmed with happiness, fun, and laughter. Every evening at 6:00 when John would walk through the door, everything changed, and we would endure the few hours his cloud hovered over us. John was like a time bomb, ready to go off at any second. We never knew what would set him off. It might be a look or an innocent slip of the tongue. Almost anything could be the catalyst to trigger his anger.

The years passed slowly, as I counted them down. Now eleven, now ten, and then nine. While I counted the years, I prayed for release from the nightmare. One afternoon I received a call from

John's physician from his job. He was required to have a physical exam to apply for a promotion. The physician asked me if I was John's wife, and I said that I was. He asked me if I could come to his office with John the next morning. Not understanding why I said that we would both be there at 8:00.

Sitting in the doctor's office with John the following morning with my 11-year-old daughter to my right, and my nine-year-old son to the left, we heard the most horrible words ever spoken in the English language. "Your husband has two months to live. He has aggressive Melanoma in the final stages. Cancer has spread to his brain, lungs, and spine. There is nothing we can do. I'm very sorry."

"Don't ever get sick. You can make me stay, but be careful that you don't get sick because I will not take care of you."

I looked over into John's terrified eyes and watched his mouth form a silent - "Please." I couldn't tell it was meant for me, or God.

We walked out of the doctor's office in a fog. It felt like a dream that we would wake up from at any moment. On the long drive home, John turned to me and said, "I know you will take me to a nursing home to die... I'm begging you not to let me die in a nursing home." The terrified look had not left his face. He searched my eyes wildly, looking for an answer. I turned around to find our children both looking at me, waiting to see what I would do. I felt the burden of this decision defining our lives and shaping our futures.

Worlds spun in those few seconds. Galaxies turned. Time turned inside out in a way I had never experienced before then. Small, hopeful eyes still looking up at me from the back seat, my mouth opened, and out spilled the words, "I'll take care of you for as long as I can."

On Halloween morning that same year, death released John from the agony of his cancer. It marked the end of the many years I had waited to be free of him. At that moment, looking down at John's lifeless body, I realized for the first time I had not been the one in chains.

We donated John's body to science with the hope of being able to mine something tangible from his death. A local college agreed to retrieve his body after the autopsy. Two days after his death, there was a knock at the door. The medical examiner who had performed John's autopsy wanted to know if I had a few minutes to talk with him. Over a cup of coffee, Dr. Pratt spread several photos out on the table and described to me the findings from the exam.

A tumor was found in John's brain, the size of a grapefruit, and by the time of his death, had pushed aside everything that was in the way of its growth. The CT scans told Dr. Pratt that the tumor had been growing for many years. "If you have noticed any extreme, abnormal behavior," he said, "it was certainly due to the slow growth of this brain tumor. You would have noticed the onset of psychological deviation 7 or 8 years ago".

Tears fell freely from my eyes as I looked down at the pictures Dr. Pratt laid out: pictures of a giant tumor in John's brain. It was this I had feared all those years, not John. The man I married was taken hostage by this horrible cancer and had to live underground while some alter ego took over, destroying all.

I don't remember saying goodbye to Dr. Pratt. I imagine he let himself out, but I don't remember him leaving. I only recall sitting and crying for hours on end, as I forgave John for the years he terrorized me. I understood that he couldn't help it.

Karen Peebles is a freelance writer living in Southern Missouri home-schooling her teenagers. A published author, Karen enjoys a simple life on her 2-acre farm where she finds inspiration to write from seeing God's hand in all things that grow around her. An ex-biker with a dozen tattoos, Karen's style of writing is sometimes rough and uncouth. Her integration into the bible-belt has been slow but steady. She attributes her metamorphosis from life on the road to a life lived to inspire others to "God's unlimited mercy which can even extend to someone like me."

Have no fear of perfection—you'll never reach it.
Salvador Dali

Dreaming Dreams and Facing Fears

By Robert B. Robeson

You gain strength, courage, and confidence by every experience in which you really stop to look fear in the face. You must do the thing you think you cannot do.

Anna Eleanor Roosevelt, Learn by Living (1960)

I remember my first dreams at the tender age of six, as the second son of a small-town Protestant minister in Truesdale, Iowa, in 1948. I distinctly recall that I wanted to be two things when I grew up: a pilot and U.S. Army officer. A yellow, single-engine Airplane often flew low over our hamlet of 125 souls. It flew so low that I could see the pilot wave back when I waved. That may have been a contributing factor to this order.

But, by this time, I'd already discovered that nightmares can be a part of our dreams, too.

One of these nightmare scenarios had occurred the previous year. My parents had left me with a farm family so that they could attend a ministerial convention in another state. While they were gone, I was taken to the top of a tall building seven miles away in Storm Lake to see the view from this new structure. The man from our church family I was staying with had picked me up and set me atop a low wall encircling the roof. With my stubby legs dangling over this lofty precipice, he pretended to push me off numerous times with fake shoves while grasping me around the waist.

It's a crisis moment that has stayed with me for over 68 years. I began to cry and fought to get down. He would never be aware of how his prank terrified me. I had an intense fear of heights from then on. This "secret" was never revealed to anyone, not even my parents until I mentioned it to my wife when I was over 50 years of age.

While growing up, I still held that dream of becoming an adventurous aviator, defying gravity and leaping tall buildings in a single bound like Superman. I continued to believe that one couldn't be a pilot and still be afraid of heights, so flying remained a mere fantasy.

I enlisted in the Oregon Army National Guard as a medical aidman at seventeen. My parents weren't pleased. My father attempted to talk me out of this decision when I asked him to sign my enlistment papers a month before high school graduation. He'd had never been in military service and had no personal reference point or experience in this regard. He eventually relented, but only grudgingly.

I served six months of basic infantry training at Ft. Ord, California and then medical aid man training at Ft. Sam Houston in San Antonio, Texas. After 2 1/2 years of college and being promoted to sergeant status, I was eligible, accepted and completed Army Infantry Officer Candidate School at Ft. Benning, Georgia and was commissioned a second lieutenant. The first part of my childhood dream was complete.

With the Vietnam conflict beginning to heat up in 1967, and with a desire to do my part, I applied for U.S. Army helicopter flight school as a medical evacuation pilot. At that point in my life, it felt like something I should do to fulfill the second part of my childhood dream. Any height above sea level was still a scary proposition for me. But for some unknown reason, it appeared to be the aviation opportunity I'd always been seeking. It was also what I felt compelled to do in spite of my chronic fear of heights. At the time of application, though, I'd vowed to myself that this weakness and fear--even if it wasn't my fault--wasn't going to diminish my dreams.

While waiting for my orders to flight school in California in 1968, I returned home to visit my parents in Oregon. My only sibling was four years older and was about to leave to be a missionary to

Nicaragua with his family. One afternoon he drove over from a neighboring town to visit me. We hadn't seen each other in years.

We stood in the middle of their living room, and he asked me what I intended to do. I told him that I was waiting for my helicopter flight school orders. I also mentioned that after graduating from this 10-month course at Ft. Wolters, Texas, and Hunter Army Airfield in Savannah, Georgia, I intended to volunteer to be a medevac pilot in Vietnam. I'll never forget his positive and encouraging words.

"You're crazy!"

"Well, I guess I am crazy because that's what I'm going to do," I replied.

I knew, even then, that the only opinion about my goals and dreams that counted was mine. Negative comments from anyone else only reflected their limitations and weren't conducive to my personal goals.

Even without negative responses from family members, this emotional decision felt like I was thrown into the middle of a shark-infested ocean without a life preserver. At the moment I'd signed my flight school application paperwork, I'd vowed to myself that this psychological challenge and fear of heights weren't going to rule or dictate my future.

My one-hour orientation flight in a flimsy-looking, open-door, OH-23D observation helicopter at Ft. Wolters in 1968 was an unnerving experience. But I believed that those who win great battles of the mind, body, and spirit must first have a dream or vision of what victory requires.

By motivating oneself to move in that direction, a person can provide a realistic way of helping to make that dream become a reality.

On March 25, 1969, I graduated as an army aviator at Hunter Army Airfield with an instrument rating. For ten trying months, my fear of heights was akin to chronic arthritis. It had the ability to cause severe pain and anxiety every day, but the only logical remedy was to press on with determination and perseverance.

Having already volunteered for combat duty, I was in the right place, at the right time, the right age, with the right skills and now with the right kind of aircraft to make an impact on other people's lives in a major way. It was an opportunity to be of service to fellow humanity even beyond my original dream.

Before three additional months elapsed, I married my fiancée and was stationed 10,000 miles from home in my first aviation assignment. Promoted to Captain, I was now Operations Officer of the 236th Medical Detachment (Helicopter Ambulance) located at Red Beach on the shore of picturesque Da Nang Harbor in Da Nang, South Vietnam.

In my one-year tour of combat duty, from July 10, 1969-July 10, 1970, I flew 987 medevac missions and helped to evacuate over 2,500 patients from both sides of the action. Seven of my helicopters were shot up by enemy fire, and I was shot down twice. It didn't take long to understand what separates the "doers" from the "dreamers" in life or some of the dangers, sacrifices, and challenges that achieving those dreams can require.

Looking back, I believe those 2,500 patients were probably thankful that I did have dreams to be a pilot and army officer and didn't listen to or become cowed by what the rest of my family thought, even if they were just concerned for my safety. Perhaps my since deceased brother was correct with his two-word judgment of my plans. Some of the exploits my fellow pilots accomplished in Vietnam probably did seem crazy to those who weren't there.

Two out of a mere total of 1,200 U.S. Army medevac pilots were awarded the Congressional Medal of Honor, one of whom I knew, among thousands of other valorous awards. But we were "our brothers' keepers," and a lot of them were counting on us. Their morale and lives depended on our flight crews being able to evacuate them quickly from the battlefield and combat chaos to a medical facility.

Collectively, we evacuated over 900,000 men, women, and children—soldiers from both sides of the action and civilians alike—during that war. What better dream could there have been than in being involved in that life-sustaining enterprise, even in the shadow of death?

Flying a helicopter into shooting situations, both day and night in all weather conditions and terrain, was like putting a mouse in the ring with an elephant. Sooner or later, that mouse is going to get stepped on no matter how brave it thinks it is. It was discovered our unarmed helicopter losses to the hostile fire were 3.3 times that of all other forms of helicopter missions in that war. As per documented on page 117 of the 1982 U.S. Army Center of Military History book, Dust Off: Army Aeromedical Evacuation in Vietnam by Peter Dorland and James Nanney.

The more hours I flew, the less altitude seemed to matter to me. After my first few months in Vietnam, I gained confidence in mastering the UH-1H (Huey) helicopter under hazardous conditions. This life and death flying helped to calm my fear of heights. There was less thought about myself and more about what displayed on our unit patch, "Striving to Save Lives."

It soon became apparent to me that love and concern for others can help conquer fear and that courage is measured by one's deeds and not by one's age, size, sex or the amount of fear one has. In this time of physical, psychological and emotional testing, I learned that overcoming fear can lead to worthwhile achievement and that you have to take risks if you're going to do anything of value in life or combat.

I've always associated medevac flying with the cartoon character Wile E. Coyote and how that Acme safe keeps dropping on his head and his Acme rocket skates continue to malfunction, time after time. He always keeps going and never gives up. One way or another, he's going to get that blasted roadrunner! That's what going after my patients, dreams and fighting my fears has been all about too.

What follows are merely a few examples from my Vietnam experiences that illustrate this point.

During August 20-22, 1969 (in less than 24 hours) my flight crew had two helicopters shot up. Our medic--Specialist Five John

N. Seebeth, III--had his larynx destroyed by AK-47 rifle fire when he was shot in the neck as we made our tactical approach into an insecure landing zone in the jungle for an infantry staff sergeant shot in the back and a leg. After we had limped back from this mission to the battalion aid station at Landing Zone Baldy, with two of our three radios also shot out, I held John's legs while Captain George Waters, Jr., MD, performed a tracheotomy without anesthesia. His wound had swollen so fast it was cutting off his airway. He somehow survived. After twelve subsequent operations, an army surgeon's skill gave him back a voice, but it wasn't the one with which we were familiar.

On September 13th, I was shot down for the first time after evacuating four wounded American infantrymen from a landing zone encircled by enemy forces.

Although our jet engine, both cyclic controls--the steering wheels of a helicopter—and various oil lines had been shot up or shot away, our bird refused to die easily. The instant I greased our skids onto the bumpy ground in an emergency running landing at Landing Zone Ross, our Lycoming engine's 1,100 horses succumbed en masse.

On Christmas morning of 1969, I was shot down for the second time, taking 19 "hits" in our cockpit, cargo compartment and one fuel cell during a supposed "ceasefire" period negotiated in Paris, France. Half an hour later my crew climbed into a replacement helicopter and returned to the same landing zone, again under heavy enemy fire. On our third attempt, we successfully evacuated nine wounded South Vietnamese Army soldiers attacked in their isolated outpost on Barrier Island, 2 miles south of Da Nang.

While evacuating seven urgent American infantrymen from an enemy minefield in early January 1970, I unknowingly set our left skid on two mines, one of which was estimated to be a 250-pound antitank mine. Neither of them detonated. An infantry lieutenant drove 40 miles in a jeep to relate this information to me a week later, or I would never have known. He said that when they blew the mines in place with C-4 explosives, the entire top of the hill disappeared.

Dealing with fear is a natural part of life. It's an undeniable experience in Combat, and it was something I learned to meet with confidence, faith, and hope. Each time a traumatic event occurred I forced myself to return immediately to the cockpit and resume flying. It wasn't just for my benefit.

Enlisted crew chiefs, medics, and my co-pilots were also watching, and it was important to take these situations in stride and not become a negative example or influence for them. I also didn't want the fear of death or heights to cause me to lose my nerve. It was important to fulfill this commitment to soldiers and civilians--on both sides of the action--who had severe wounds, their own fears, and who were hurting far more than myself. I often think of what I would have missed in helping others in life if my fear of heights had been allowed to overwhelm me, or if I hadn't followed my dreams. Sometimes, we have to endure tough times in life before we can truly appreciate the good times.

Through years of struggle, I've learned that fears surround all of us, along with challenges and opportunities as we chase our dreams. If I had only helped to save one life in those 987 combat missions, and hundreds of other medevac missions in West Germany from 1970-1974 with the 63rd Medical Detachment in Landstuhl, it still would have been worth the effort. I would willingly return all of my medals and go through combat all over again if I could erase just one name from the black granite wall of the Vietnam Veterans Memorial in Washington, DC.

To be truthful, my anxiety about heights, from that traumatic experience in Iowa as a five-year-old, 68 years ago, hasn't completely disappeared. This original dread just no longer controls me. This fear, which frightened me most was the same one that proved to be exhilarating when I fought my way past it. I've discovered that what may seem to be the worst possible thing that can occur in life can sometimes turn out to be positive after all. Perhaps acrophobia has been more of a "gift" to me than anything else. I might not have accomplished what I have in life if this fear hadn't spurred my flying dream.

My 73-year journey on this spinning ball of clay has been one in which I've learned to make a variety of fears my companions. They have stretched my understanding of life. I've become more sympathetic toward others and have lost my impatience regarding those who have their distinct anxieties and fears to deal with their "little bag of rocks" to pack around.

I've found it's not helpful to be so entangled in fears of failure or calamity that I wind up immobilized. Our experiences in life, when we confront our fears, can be like exquisite jewels or fine paintings. They can inspire and bring joy to ourselves and our fellow travelers.

There was a saying among helicopter jockeys in Vietnam that I often recall. "Helicopter pilots don't fly. They just beat the air into submission." I've reminded myself of this many times, since then, and continue to apply this philosophy when fear of any sort attempts to invade my mind, heart or world.

Vietnam also taught me to be stronger than I thought I was. It helped me to live out my flying dreams, which lasted nineteen years and allowed life to take me to a place where I was meant to be. Also, I learned never to be afraid to give my very best, even when I was fearful and in jeopardy of dying myself. I've found it's important to understand that what we feel, fear and experience in life has been felt, feared and experienced by others seeking to fulfill their dreams.

Our challenges and anxieties aren't unique. They've all been faced and overcome by other people. When our fears are allowed to overwhelm our dreams, life seems smudged through cloudy spectacles. Excuses for feeling these fears may appear to be legitimate, but they're still excuses. Fear's control of us can be diminished, sometimes eliminated, by doing, over and over, that which is feared.

Motivated people discover that it's possible to do more than they believe they can. It merely means removing the limits on their vision. This leap of faith demands painstaking effort and diligence.

These qualities help lift those black shrouds of fear, anxiety, and insecurity that continually tempt many to discard their dreams.

On June 2, 1995, Air Force Captain Scott O'Grady was shot out of the sky in his F-16C jet fighter in Bosnia by a Serbian ground-to-air missile. He escaped and evaded for six days before being rescued by a U.S. Marine helicopter crew. I was watching his first TV interview at my home in Lincoln, Nebraska when he surprisingly admitted, "I didn't want to punch-out because I'm afraid of heights." This admission made me smile. It was obvious that I hadn't been the only aviator who has had to deal with this fear.

For doers and fear-fighters who never give up, success is bound to follow. Your dreams will realize.

It's like trying to hit the ground when your jet engine is shot out at 1,500 feet. You can't miss. I should know.

Robert B. Robeson has been published 870 times in 320 publications in 130 countries. He's also been awarded eight decorations for valor from the American and South Vietnamese governments. Retiring as a lieutenant colonel, after a 27-year military career as a helicopter medical evacuation pilot on three continents and combat in Vietnam, he served as a newspaper managing editor and columnist. Robeson has a BA in English from the University of Maryland-College Park and has completed extensive undergraduate and graduate work in journalism at the University of Nebraska-Lincoln. He lives in Lincoln, Nebraska with his wife of 46 years, Phyllis

---

"The Pilot that Weathered the Storm"

And oh! If again, the rude whirlwind should rise,
The dawning of peace should fresh darkness deform,
The regrets of the good and the fears of the wise
Shall turn to the Pilot that weathered the Storm.

George Canning (1802)

The Flood

By Nicole Pinkman

I awakened abruptly, and all I could hear were screams. At first, I could not decipher the voice, but as the glaze of sleep cleared from my eyes, I realized it was my mom shouting.

"The house is getting flooded, climb on your wardrobe!"

Suddenly, I felt a floating sensation. As I tried to see what was going on, I realized water had flooded our house.

Fear gripped me immediately. On instinct, I climbed down my bed. The water was neck deep. I tried to maneuver to the door, but it stayed firmly closed. The force of the water prevented me from opening it.

It was at this point that I realized my mom was screaming from the other side of the door, telling me to get up on top of my wardrobe, above the water level.

But I was so overwhelmed with fear to process that information. The only thing in my mind was to try and get out of the room; to try and get to my mom. I pulled and pulled on the door to no avail. That was when I began to cry. I just stood and stared at the door, while the water level kept rising.

I was shivering as the cold water had seeped through my clothing and the air penetrated my body. This moment seemed to take forever, I couldn't move, and with each passing moment, I cried louder.

After a while, the water level threatened to overcome me. It was then the instinct for survival kicked in. I tried to make my way through the water to see if could reach my wardrobe and climb it.

But I couldn't make it. I didn't know how to swim, but I managed to keep pushing on with my eyes closed.

Finally, I touched something that looked like a knob. Gathering all the strength I could muster, I grabbed it and pushed myself up. As my head came out of the water, in that split second, I made out where the wardrobe was.

The water sucked me back in.

This time, I pulled on the knob with so much force, as I came out, I grabbed a second handle, which luckily for me, supported my weight. From there, I was able to reach out and climb my wardrobe.

Once on top of the wardrobe, shivering and overcome with fear, I heard my mom's screams. I'll never quite know how I made it to the top.

As I huddled myself there, the water level kept rising. Terrified doesn't even begin to describe how I felt. Finally, the door opened, and I saw a man in a military uniform wave to me, with my mom right behind him. I couldn't wave back; I just stayed stiff. Being tall, he navigated what was the almost waist-high water to him much easier than I had been able to. He reached me with determination, and lifted me from where I was and then we all made our way arduously through the rising levels of water in the house, to the outside.

I would learn later a horrible, record-breaking hurricane had hit our area. The flooding of the river-way we lived upon was either filling up or sweeping house after house all around us, away. Somehow, ours was still standing.

Right about where the edge of our yard once was, a rescue boat sat waiting for us. The man waved my mom into the boat with the help of the others already in it. Then he lifted me into the safety of my mother's arms. Her face was red and filled with tears. She just held me in a tight embrace, weeping.

I was three years old and the mental images of the day still lingered as if it happened yesterday.

In my experience, while growing up, I learned that a lot of things motivate us. I once conducted a survey as part of my thesis during my days of studying psychology. The aim of the survey was to find out what motivates a certain group of people. The results of the survey showed that an overwhelming 85% of the respondents claimed fear motivations of one sort or another.

There is nothing in this world that makes us more uncomfortable than fear, which has many faces: the fear of injury, of death, of disease, of pain, of missing an opportunity, of being rejected, of being scammed, of failure, etc. Built into us, we have the flight or fight response, and when we face a threat or challenge so difficult it threatening, our response system is configured to choose the safest path, usually one of the least resistant.

Often, the initial urge is to flee, or in some way escape the discomfort. We want to reach a place that is familiar and comfortable. A place that feels safe, and we feel more in control.

Business marketers understand the innate psychology behind fear, and they use it to trap us. They paint a situation that invokes a sense of fear in us, and then they offer a solution—that path of least resistance to our comfort zone—which is often by using their products and services.

Food, fashion and beauty products marketing attempts to manipulate us every day; dozens, if not hundreds of times through television, the internet, even at the supermarket. This conditioning is so much the cultural norm it is a completely accepted aspect of modern life – circumstances that would have felt completely foreign just a few decades ago.

We are repeatedly bombarded with how using this product, or that one can help us overcome our problems. Indeed, we have been conditioned. Thus, we find ourselves spending our money on unnecessary products, from soaps to vitamins, steroids, weight loss pills, and anti-aging creams, etc. Most of these things were considered unnecessary just a few decades back.

But we are smart to realize the problem itself is often created, painted and fed by the marketers behind the products they are selling as the solution.

Then there is this idea. Fear, while being a powerful motivational tool, negates us and our sense of importance.

Question: would you prefer to use fear to motivate your kids to perform well in school? Or is there a better or, stronger motivator. A more positive one.

After analyzing my thesis, I came up with the conclusion that fear, while being a powerful motivator is nothing but negative emotions: ones that are unhealthy, dangerous, and that slowly kill. And yes, there is, in fact, a better motivator than fear.

Encouragement

Humans, as opposed to most other creatures, have an amazing capacity to allow the want of something we perceive as better to outpace our fear.

From my story, I lived with the fear of water for almost 18 years because of my experience with the flood as a kid. After attending a life-changing seminar by a motivational speaker, I decided it was time to face my fear.

I registered in a local swimming club and took classes. At first, images of that event flooded my brain whenever I was in the water. I would have flashes of that horrible day. But I was determined. I kept training and developing both my swimming skills and my mindset. I decided to let go and stop clinging to events that are in my past.

I wanted to succeed so badly; I wanted to be a good swimmer.

In the beginning, before swimming practice, I sometimes cried because of the mental images, the fear that I had to overcome, once and for all. Slowly, I began to let go of all the limiting thoughts which had held me back for so long.

I used that fear to challenge myself; I realized if I could overcome this—I could do almost anything! And it worked.

I not only overcame my fear of the water, but I also became a good swimmer. I even competed a bit with a swim team in college. This experience was a beautiful, empowering one I would never forget.

So, I want to encourage us, to let go of our fears. We can achieve more and do more if we can overcome the fear of anything that has trapped us in a shell of self-pity and confusion.

One of the ways we can start overcoming is to keep telling ourselves positive things. Say it loud, say it every day. Tell yourself you are a champion and no obstacle can stop you from achieving your dream. Surround yourself with positive people that will help develop your faith. Envision your success—daily. Several times each day even!

Sometimes I ask, 'What if Thomas Edison, out of fear of failure, having tried for more than 10,000 times gave up the idea of the light bulb?" We might still be living in darkness.

Another fear mnemonic is False Evidence Appearing Real.

Those things you tell yourself that discourage you are not real. Who says you are not beautiful? Who says you can't get married? Who says you cannot be anything you want to be? Who would have thought America would have a black president? Who would have thought, a blind person can play the piano and become one of the greatest songwriters? Who would have thought a deaf person can compose wonderful symphonies?

It's all in the mind. Develop your faith, rid false evidence trying to become part of your reality, and say no to your fears.

Nicole Pinkman is a professional freelance/ creative writer. Find her at: https://www.linkedin.com/pub/nicole-pinkman/106/aa1/b53

We can easily forgive a child who is afraid of the dark;
the real tragedy of life is when a man is afraid of the light.

Plato.

Perfect

By Christina Hamlett

As it always did, her anger became a scalding fury. "I could have you put away for life!" she screamed, repeatedly jabbing me in the chest with her index finger. "I could have you put someplace you'll never get out!" She was breathless with undisguised rage, and the chill that hung on the edge of her words made me realize she had every intention of making good on her favorite threat. As she was always so fond of saying, it would be her word against mine and no one—not even my own father—would come to my defense.

I was only 17, and my latest "crime" was to try to break up with my dumb-as-a-rock boyfriend. Why couldn't my mother be like other girls' mothers and simply applaud my choice? Obviously, of course, it was because other girls' mothers didn't have a dark agenda. George was crazy about my mother and vice versa. A little too crazy. She'd buy him new clothes and ask him to model them. They'd stop laughing whenever I came in the room, and she'd whisper—loudly enough for me to hear—"We'll continue this later." When George one day confided in her that I was unwilling to "prove" my love for him, she told him it was all right if he ever wanted to use force. She then told me that if I were to become pregnant, she'd throw us the perfect wedding with lots of presents.

Where was my father in all of this? Usually retreating behind his Wall Street Journal. What few times I tried to enlist his support, he'd tell me I was exaggerating. A part of me wondered whether he was as afraid of her as I was or if it was love that had blinded him to the sadistic side of her personality.

Now and again I try to remember if there was a particular moment when I first knew she was mentally ill. It wasn't a thing talked about in the 50s and 60s and certainly not in wealthy circles. I wore the best clothes; I had the best toys, and I had the perfect little princess bedroom. As long as I stayed in line and kept under the radar, I was safe from her alcohol-induced outbursts. "If you really loved me," she'd say, "you'd do exactly what I want." She said the same thing to my father, which usually precipitated an outpouring of expensive gifts that she would enjoy for a while and then discard out of boredom.

As I got older, I realized she was having trouble keeping her stories straight. I'd remind her of things she said, and she would testily snap that I was a liar, and she had said no such thing. It was pointless to argue with her. If I did, she'd threaten to cut off my allowance and have me thrown out in the street. "And don't think you could tell anyone, like your teachers or your friends' parents because it will be my word against yours." Money became her all-purpose control mechanism. "I could disown you!" she'd threaten. She took extreme pride in reminding me that my father was going to leave everything to her but that none of their combined wealth would come to me when she died if I didn't do exactly what she wanted.

She was forever contriving sick plots against people she felt had wronged her, especially her own mother. Many a time when the latter came to visit us, my mother would muse about what a terrible thing it would be if the elderly woman accidentally fell down the stairs. I was aghast that she'd even think of this. In response, she'd laugh and say, "I'll just tell the police that you're the one who gave her a push. The worst that could happen is you'll spend a few years in juvie. But don't worry, your father and I will come and visit you." I made a deliberate point to go overnight with friends so I would be nowhere near the house if such a horrible accident transpired.

She became obsessed with staying young and having her hair done twice a week to keep it perfectly blond. She bought clothes better suited to someone half her age. I lived in fear that my friends would see her, and I'd be a laughingstock. I look back and wonder why I didn't confront her behavior rather than try to stay invisible as much as possible. The reason, of course, is always the same; I was afraid she'd do even more damage and attempt to harm me physically. Psychologically, it was her aim to destroy my self-confidence and self-esteem. She tried to impress upon me that I'd never become a success as a writer and that I would never be as beautiful as she was. "Even your father thinks you're a miserable failure," she said. I'd look in his direction, hoping against hope that he'd speak up. He knew better, though, than to challenge anything she declared the truth.

When I made the decision at age 19 to move out, her toxic response was "Good riddance." She couldn't believe I had landed a well-paying job and that I was moving into a studio apartment. She predicted I'd last no more than a week and would beg her to let me come home. When I turned the key in the front door of that first apartment, I was resolved not only never to go back but also to minimize my contact with her. Sadly, that also meant minimizing contact with my father who had let me down in so many unfortunate ways.

In 2007, word reached me through some friends of my father that my mother had been diagnosed with Alzheimer's. Since he could no longer care for her himself, he had located the best nursing facility for her and then made an odd request of the administration. He would be moving into the same room with her. Even though there was nothing medically wrong with him, he was afraid she'd be lonely if he weren't there to keep her company. The staff reminded him that she didn't even know who he was. That made no difference. He wanted to be there just for those fleeting moments when she seemed to come "back" to him. He refused to take meals in the dining room or even to go out for walks.

He wrote me a letter and asked me to visit. "We can be a family again," he said. I had not seen either of them in almost 30 years, but the pain and the fear still lingered in the back corners of my mind. He had kept silent during all the times I needed him. I saw the call for reconciliation for what it was; he was just lonely. I wished him well but let him know that we would not see each other again in this lifetime.

When she passed away three years later, I learned that she had never made a will. Accordingly, a portion of her estate—much against her wishes, I'm sure—came to me. My father made another appeal for us to get together. Again, I refused. At the time of her passing, the nursing home administrators expected him to leave. "No," he told them, "I think Claire would like me to stay right here where we spent our final years together." Even beyond the grave, she still had a stranglehold on his heart.

Two years ago, he finally joined her and—as the sole heir—everything came into my possession. I flip back through the family albums, and I try to find clues as to how a mother could be so cruel and hateful toward her only child. In the pictures, though, the three of us are always smiling. It's the problem with pictures, for they only capture the perfection. "We're the perfect family," she always boasted. "Absolutely perfect."

I think back to all of the opportunities I had to contest this observation, to give voice to my anger and frustration, even to suggest that she get professional help for her crazy state of mind. Then I remember how powerless a child is to do anything except to keep quiet and stay out of the way.

In the end, it was my own fear that probably saved my life.

Former actress and director Christina Hamlett is an award-winning author and media relations expert whose credits to date include 32 books, 158 stage plays, and hundreds of articles and interviews that appear online and in trade publications worldwide. She is also a script consultant for the film business and a professional ghostwriter. www.authorhamlett.com.

Fear is only as deep as the mind allows.

Japanese Proverb

The Carnival Ride

By Connie Kerbs

I was five years old in the mid-1970's when my father took me to my first Carnival. I still remember the pretty lights and all the exciting sounds and smells of that experience. After passing through the ticket booth area, we weaved through the crowds while I enjoyed the view atop his strong, young shoulders.

It wasn't long before I was working on a sticky ball of pink cotton candy that melted in my mouth while he took me on a couple of kiddie rides. I remember pointing to one of the bigger ones a little further into the bright, noisy landscape that seemed to shrink and mute us.

"The zipper?!" my dad said in a tone, half playful, half serious. He tried to talk me out of it, and then reluctantly agreed to check it out. I think he thought I would chicken out.

Not this girl! Not when I was with my dad. He was my superhero. I thought he could do anything. And I was fearless—because he was.

We reached the strange piece of engineering, essentially forming an X, made of two long perpendicular beams, each with a larger basket at one end, and a slightly smaller one at the other.

The beams spun in opposite directions, whirling around an axis on either side. This contraption seemed pretty simple compared to some of the other rides that were running all around this part of the carnival. And, by the sounds of the excited screams coming from the larger baskets—it would be tremendous fun!

As we approached the gate, the people before us crawled out of the cage-like shapes. Up close, they didn't look like they had too much fun. One person limped around the back of the ride area still hunched over, and from the sounds of it, "tossed their cookies," as my grandmother called it. Another was acting dizzy. Still, the curiosity was too much for me. Besides, my brave, strong dad was there.

As we waited, he tried once more to talk me out of it. He was either teasing or he had acquiesced to let the life lesson teach itself to his determined little girl. Maybe some of both. Of course, even he couldn't have guessed what was about to happen to us.

It was finally our turn! I climbed in the apparatus, surprised at how squirrelly the cage felt. My dad climbed in after me, which made it swing and sway even more. The smelly attendant gave instructions about our safety belts. Then he impatiently lifted over the bar like mechanism that fastened down upon our upper legs. Well, it fastened properly on my dad, but my legs were too scrawny, and the gap between my small knees and the bar was almost humorous.

I had some trouble with my buckle, so my dad reached over to help. It seemed uncooperative with him at first, too, but my dad could fix anything. Soon I was set, and ready for the ride of my life.

The ride started out slowly, but quickly sped up. My young, inexperienced self was caught off-guard with how much time we spent flying through the air upside down, sideways or just spinning in all different directions at once. It was one thing watching it from the ground. It had looked so fun! Suddenly, not so much anymore.

I will never be quite sure how, when or why it happened. As the ride reached full speed of hurling us through the air, I suddenly felt myself flying *through* the contained space. Before either of us could figure out what had happened, I was on the opposite side of the cage from my father, with back to him, looking down at the ant sized people below, momentarily pinned by the spin's inertia.

I could hear myself screaming—not the fun kind, but the kind when you're terrified for your very life. And I was. As was my father, by the look on his suddenly 'not having fun' face I finally saw when the forces threw me another direction, uncontrollably.

As I slammed back toward him to the other side of the cage; he did his best to grab onto me. We just kept whirling and spinning, with moments of floating between the sensations of being tossed, with unimaginable force, side to side, back and forth, and upside down. At first, it was the best he could do to get a grip on my legs, as my top half hit the red, metal netting of the cage supposedly designed to contain us—several times, and hard!

I clutched for dear life onto the metal caging that shelled the baskets, and which had just room for my small fingers to claw. My dad yelled, to no avail, for the attendant to stop it. I was too scared to scream after a while. I just clung desperately onto whatever grip I got on the wiring. In my dad's getting a hold on me and keeping me from flailing loose with the upside-down spins, the bar that had fastened down his legs had popped up, too.

That was when he realized the error of his ways for not doing his seat belt either. Probably because he had been distracted by trying to help with mine—which obviously hadn't worked.

The two of us jarred around loosely, like rattles in a baby toy. We were thrown every which way in what became an ordeal of horror, him trying to steady himself while holding onto me, and me holding onto the little holes of wiring that formed the top half of the see-thru basket-like cages. I could feel the sting of my fingers as they clawed at the thin, red, woven metal until they were numb.

My dad must have found a way to brace himself with his feet, as he held tightly onto the bottom half of me, in the best efforts possible to keep me from body slamming all around and side to side, not too unlike an egg being scrambled. I was not aware of much else, except that I was beyond terrified. I felt like a rag doll.

When the torture finally stopped, after what seemed an eternity, my dad just held me, and I sobbed uncontrollably. My fingers throbbed from the bruising and abrasions caused by my gripping at the thin, metal framework so intensely.

With me still clutching him tightly, my dad didn't wait until the attendant let us out of our would-be death trap. That was when he realized how easily the door could've just popped open. It only took the slightest push, and it opened from the inside. That was when I saw the look of deep anger enhance the cloud of worry that had defined my dad's face moments before. As we climbed out of that terrifying experience, I was grateful for the firm, non-moving ground.

My dad gave the attendant a piece of his fury, then tracked down someone in charge to tell about the non-functioning seatbelt, failed safety- bar, and the joke of a safety latch on the cage's door.

It was some time before I could ride *any* Carnival rides again, and then only cautiously. Eventually, my teen friends would tease me about my reluctance (okay, total avoidance) of thrill-rides.

To this day, when my kids or I ride, seatbelts, fastener bars, and door safety latches are inspected mercilessly. And that's just the kiddie rides. When I feel extra brave, I work up to the merry-go-round.

Forty-plus years later, I still think of my dad, and how, despite any oversights made, he did his best in this unexpected, frightening situation. After all, he never once let me go during the whole ordeal.

In fact, all of this left more than one imprint upon me. Of course, there are real dangers of rides to respect. But there is more. I learned a definition of bravery. It's like this: sometimes you don't have time to think, or problem solve. All you can do is instinctively respond.

While not perfect, brave people get through difficult situations the best way possible, sometimes terrified all the while. But they do it, just like my dad, who somehow, kept me from jostling to my demise that day. Also like him, they get to the other side of such a time capsule - still brave, but older, wiser, and perhaps more cautious.

"Life is what happens to us while we are making other plans."
Allen Saunders

Choice Not Circumstance

By Tina Jensen

Last night I cried myself to sleep. Two days ago, I was writing a story about feeling confident in walking around my house naked, now that I was living by myself after 39 years. Today, I need to contemplate walking the employment agency path, as for the first time in all these years, I've been made redundant.

This morning I woke up bleary eyed and began the grieving process all over again. Sadness. Anger. Emptiness. Tears welled up once more, my lungs squeezing hard. I felt the weight of rent payments, new car tires, medical bills, and uncertainty sit upon my shoulders, fastening me down.

Normally one who torpedoes through life with, some would say, an irrational level of optimism, I was faltering. Along with my long-held view 'cannot' should be banned from the dictionary, I added outsourcing. Redundancy should be a swear word.

This afternoon, I considered how much of my time, energy, commitment, and skills had been exhausted over a ten month period. I decided rather than continuing my day curled up in a fetal position and sobbing through the anguished thoughts of the purpose of my journey; I would head down to my local beach and just sit. I didn't want to think anymore. I was choosing to let it go: the situation was out of my control, and I just wanted to spend the time focused on positive outcomes. Polishing my resume as job searching had been all-consuming for so long. Reflection, acknowledgment, and acceptance of the future needed its place too.

En route to the tranquility of waves and feet immersed in warm sand, I passed an advertising sign: choice, not circumstance determines your success.

As I sat and observed the seagulls, boats, fishers and kite surfers, I contemplated the intention of the sign, and how choosing courage over fear could support me through this period. My last 24 hours ran through my head like a showreel.

I saw courage in the supermarket where I observed the mother ahead of me deny her child the temptation of check-out goodies.

I respected a friend's courage to commit to changing his mindset, despite the difficult child custody case embroiling within.

I recalled the courage of a Cambodian farmer who tilled his land, fully aware that the impending rainy season could destroy his crops.

I appreciated courage when I hung up the phone from an inspiring young man who has followed his dream to make a difference, putting himself into huge debt at the same time. I flipped through photographs in my mind that reminded me of the physical pain of courage when each night I bandaged my blistered feet after walking kilometers of the Great Wall of China.

The same photo album reminded me that in some of the most impoverished countries, I've seen courage and survival co-exist.

I felt courage when I sat in the darkness, feeling the emotions from so much in my life that has saddened and disrupted my focus on the positive and shifting forward. Courage is to allow these feelings to work in you and your life, but not allowing them to be a permanent state.

I know I have courage when I reflect on the curve balls my life has thrown and the commitment I have shown to overcome them.

Most of us talk about courage regarding actions or devastating circumstances. In a tough situation, there is little one can do but survive with all the patience and strength you can dig up from within.

For me, the real test of courage is more than simply putting up with a bad situation. The sign of a courageous person is one who can recognize fear, and with mind and spirit, makes a committed choice to continue forward, even if it means first taking a few steps back.

Courage is something that more of us need to develop in our daily lives. We should not have to wait until a point of desperation to dig it out. Courage creates visions, it gives us foresight, it moves us forward, it gives us focus, and it develops commitment.

Circumstance need not determine one's life. The choice of courage is a powerful one.

I think I can; I think I can, I think I can. I know I can, I know I can, I know I can. I did it.

Tina Jensen is a world traveler, wellness coach, author and kindle of www.createnoordinarylife.com, a movement borne of the need to be inspired, passionate, challenged and satisfied. Full of ideas, feelings, and experiences, she can often be found simply being still, listening internally and observing outwardly. Tina sees the world through a rare kaleidoscopic lens of experience, empathy, and awe. She is passionate about sharing real stories of ordinary people committed to the pursuit of dreams, extinguishing the mundane, overcoming challenges and feeling compelled to make a difference, either to their own life or those of others. She simply wants you to say yes.

You must never be fearful of what you are doing when it is right.
Marie Curie

Iron Ana

By Ana Hernández Millán

When I was a child, my favorite tale was "John without Fear," or "Iron John." When other little girls dreamt of fairy tales and princess stories I always fantasized about Iron John, the man without any fear. That story had left an imprint on my personality and character.

Three years ago, I fainted walking up the metro stairs, and I knew it was serious. Some years previous to this episode I had been very ill, but all the medical tests that had been run by very expert doctors were inconclusive, and it was all believed to be heavy stress.

When I collapsed in the metro I knew whatever it was I had, it was back. I started visiting doctors and doctors; all of them seemed unable to understand my very unusual blood test results. Finally, one of the doctors I visited took the time to listen to me, and disregarded the standard procedures and started medical treatments.

Over the next several months, I lost the capacity to read. I could see the letters, but my brain was unable to make any sense of them. That was when I got scared. I thought that even if I were supposedly too young for a degenerative mental disease, it could be that…

Then other symptoms followed. I could not stand up more than 2 minutes, or my blood pressure would suddenly drop so that I would faint. After one of these crises, it could take weeks for my blood pressure to return to a normal range so that I could walk around again.

In the middle of my health ordeal, my mom was diagnosed with cancer. This was so unexpected, and I was scared to lose her, too.

We went through all this, and while my mom recovered her health, I did not. I have spent the last year and a half unable to have a normal life, unable to stand up for more than 2 minutes. I take about thirty different pills per day. I feel like I live at the doctors, visiting all the possible physicians who might have some solutions. I was lucky in that two of them from two different countries decided I was worth trying to make some progress. They went the extra mile, and they had been working together trying to find a solution for me with a language barrier between them, as they speak different languages.

Somehow in the middle of it, all my health problems just suddenly improved. Then, just as suddenly, when we ran the last blood test one of my doctors called me to say that they were catastrophic. Nothing seemed to work, and it was time to take a different approach.

When I started suffering from this disease and I was first misdiagnosed as having heavy stress, I went to Cusco (Peru). If stress was the cause of it, at that moment, I decided I needed a complete change of life. I left the corporate world with all of its demands, its competition, and its long working hours. Instead, I volunteered with a very creative children's project in the ancient capital of the Inca Empire.

Of the three months I spent there, I was sick for six weeks, but it was an incredible experience. A few months after that first trip and, before I collapsed in the metro, I returned to the very same place in Cusco. That was when my doctor called me to say my last blood results were worse than "my normal" and that we needed to take some different approach. We went through my blood results for the last five years trying to find something we missed; something that might offer some answers. We discovered that the two times I had been in Peru my blood results had been almost back to normal.

We did some medical research following this discovery and found something compelling. The high altitudes of places like Cusco could generate metabolic changes. The ancient capital of the Inca Empire sits at 3,400 meters above sea level, just over 11,000 feet. Some unique cases, similar to mine had found this to be beneficial.

The question is: Do you go to a third world country to get healed just by being over there when in my actual health condition a gastro infection can potentially kill me?

I came to the decision of returning to Cusco in June of this year, and I gave myself some months to improve my overall condition in what by now has become "my normal" which is a very limiting condition for a 44-year-old woman.

In ten days, I will be landing in Cusco where I am to spend six months. They say my body needs two months to adjust to the altitude and then some more months are needed to gain the full benefits. That is if I am fortunate enough that this risky approach works.

I am scared to death, to tell you the truth, to jump in the first of the three planes that will be taking me from my home to Cusco. It is more than a thirty-hour trip. I will be leaving behind my family, my friends, my home, my doctors, the easy things that we take for granted in the first world. Things like a hot shower, heating, hygienic conditions, and safety in the streets.

In ten days, I will be leaving behind all I know, and I will be jumping into the unknown, hoping it will work.

Fear. It's that feeling, emotion or thought that stops us from doing something. This something usually implies some big change in our life: changing jobs, getting married or divorced, moving away, allowing ourselves to be ourselves. Having a baby or retiring.

When I take that first plane, I will have in front of me a white canvas to be filled in with new experiences, new people, and places. I know I may be back, and some of my dear family may no longer be here because of their elderly conditions. Or, I may never see my home or loved ones again. I may not make it. This trip may be just a one-way ticket. The simple flu could mean the end.

It comes to this: fear is a choice which confronts us in life.

Now, I think of my favorite childhood story, Iron John. I have never allowed fear to run my life. I focus on staying positive, and not dwelling on the *would-be's*, and the unknowns.

I don't know much, but I know this. You can't allow your fears to win the battle, whatever battle you are fighting. You have to be in charge, not your fears! Even in the middle of the most complicated situation, remember: fear is just a creation of your mind and your set of beliefs. Our mind creates the fear, and so it can also create courage. The choice is always yours.

Please wish me good luck. I am doing my best to choose! I am doing as Iron John would do, and choosing courage.

Note: The Grimms Fairy Tale, "Iron John," also goes by, " John without Fear, and sometimes, "The Story of the Youth Who Went Forth to Learn What Fear Was. It is also known by, " Iron Hans," published in 1812 and 1819, by the Brothers Grimm. It explains the story of John, a boy who did not know what fear was and who never shuddered. As he always wanted to know these things, John accepted the challenge of spending three nights in an enchanted castle where the most horrific things happened. He had a great reward from the King for accepting and meeting the challenge.

Ana Hernández Millán was born in Barcelona (Spain) and lives in Brussels (be.linkedin.com/in/anahernandezmillan). After a successful corporate career she turned to non-profit causes, she runs a small Belgian NGO focusing on children's issues in the high Andes of Peru (http://chaka-runa.org). She is fighting an unusual disease but hopes to be an inspirational writer.

How much pain they have cost us, the evils which never happened.
Thomas Jefferson

Brush it off Darlin'

By Mary Law Meinelt

I stood, frozen in fear, at the foot of my parents' bed. The moonlight flowing through the windows spreads a faint and mysterious glow across their bed, illuminating the blood that's spilled over my mother as she held the neck of a broken liquor bottle in her hand. The blow to Daddy's skull was all that stopped the onslaught of his fists to her face. Their bodies then become silhouettes, moving in slow motion. I heard my mother whimpering. The glue of fear held me very still until a child's instinct of danger pushed me to run.

Terrified, I ran down a well-worn path surrounded by towering weeks. They hovered over me, enveloping me like giant Venus Fly-traps. The fear that a thing, some invisible monster I knew was there, will pluck me up propelled my tiny legs, making them churn faster. The memory ends and begins to repeat itself. No matter how hard I try to dredge up more about that night, I can't. The next day my mother is gone and my grandmother, Mammy. I felt something enveloping me as I tried to outrun it in the dark. The dim light from the tenant house at the end of the path encouraged me to continue my escape.

The memory ended and began repeating itself. Still, no matter how hard I try to dredge up more about that night, I couldn't. The next day my mother was gone and my grandmother, Mammy, was the only one there.

When I was twenty-seven, Dr. Proctor, a psychiatrist, asked me, "Mary, what was your first memory?" His question was like a stick hitting a piñata, spilling out this dark memory, instead of bright, colorful candies. With deep sobs, tears rushing down my face, mixing with mucus running out of my nose, I caught my breath and told him what I believed to be the story of my first memory of my life. Did it happen exactly like this? Did it happen at all?

When I told her bits and pieces, she'd always tell me it was my imagination, and that it was impossible for me to remember anything that happened in Hopkins because we'd move to Summerton, South Carolina when I was four. Sometimes, she'd laugh and tell me, "You're being dramatic, Sarah." She often called me Sarah after the famous actress, Sarah Bernhardt.

But, I could see our little white house that sat in the middle of a pecan orchard. I saw myself as a tiny little girl, running, always running down a path toward the tenant house.

Did I run out of the house to keep my daddy from hurting—even killing my mother? Maybe not exactly as I saw it happen, but I am so sure of my memory I must travel from my home in Winston-Salem, North Carolina, to Columbia to visit my parents. I must talk to my mother. I must find out.

Shortly after I arrived, I told my mother there was something I needed to ask her and will she please come with me where we can be private. I wanted her to confirm that my memory did happen, that these bits and pieces that escaped from my subconscious were not my imaginations as she'd always said they were.

She followed me into the living room, and we stopped in the middle of the room. We stood close, facing each other. All the familiar furnishings, the sofa by the wall, Daddy's chair by the window, faded into the background, leaving us alone in the center of the room. I didn't sit down. I was too anxious to hear her answer to my question.

I insisted I did remember Daddy beating her. I was desperate for her to explain it to me, determined to prove to myself that I had not made up this memory. It was real. It happened. I looked into her soft blue-gray eyes through her glasses with large frames, and in a soft and gentle voice, I said, "Please, Mother, I need to know. I remember that night in Hopkins. Please tell me what happened."

"It's just your imagination."

My eyes beg as I look into hers.

A minute passed by and then in a low, deliberate voice; she told me her story, a story about the beating she endured that night. It spilled from the deepest recesses of her soul, a beating so severe her left eye still droops as evidence. As the described that night, she took her hand and with her fingers, pulled the flesh beneath her eye down so far her entire face was freakishly distorted. Her voice, almost a growl, expresses the deep anger that erupted from years of silence.

"He beat me, the drunk. Your daddy was a mean drunk. I reached over and grabbed his liquor bottle and hit his head as hard as I could to stop him. He knocked my eye out of its socket. I was in the hospital for three weeks."

And then, in a quick gesture, she threw her hands into the air, brushes her shoulder as if to brush off a bug and says, "What does it matter?" And in a voice full of resignation she said, "Too late now. Brush it off darlin'." She shrugged her shoulders, threw her hands in the air, and ends with another, "Brush it off."

Gently, I wrapped my arms around my fragile mother in an attempt to console her. I felt her pain overwhelming me.

For a moment, just a moment, she let me hold her as I whispered, "I'm so sorry." Tears came to my eyes, but not to hers. My mother doesn't cry. She is brave and stoic. But she allowed me to share this memory with her, one that has haunted me. We do not need to talk about the damage that night had done to each of us, mother and child. We both knew.

Her great pain overshadowed my suffering. It sent any of mine slithering from the light, back into darkness.

She pulled away, "Mary Elizabeth, you were too young. You couldn't remember." She places a period to the memory, similar to The End that flashes to tell you the movie is over and to leave the theater now.

But it is not the end for me. There are other memories that fed my fears of night, especially in the country when I am isolated, away from lights and people. I know it's a fear I will never completely shed, but I've learned how to handle my physical reaction to it. I've learned not to allow it to cripple me so that I can enjoy the beauty of the country.

While the small bits of memory I have of my years in Hopkins were few, it seemed now that our days were full of the sunshine, butterflies fluttering from wildflower to wildflower in the backyard, as birds flew from tree to tree. There was a quiet gentleness to the day, a feeling of calm, but not so the nights. It is only with retrospection that I believe that being a girl and four years younger than my brother offered me a kind of insulation from Daddy's brutality when he was drunk. Daddy wanted to toughen my brother, make a man out of him.

It is another memory that suggests this perhaps was an underlying part of my brother's mental illness years later. It took place in the living room of our little white house that sits in the middle of a pecan orchard. It was a stormy night.

Through the living room windows, I saw sharp lightning streak through the night sky, followed by rolling thunder. The wind, clanging barn doors and my brother's cries from a storm inside our house that matched the one outside. Daddy clutched Teddy's arm as Teddy begged, "Pleeease. Please don't make me. Pleeease."

Daddy slapped Teddy, who tries to duck. The blow landed on Teddy's face. When Teddy tried to pull away, Daddy gripped his arm and shoved him toward the kitchen. A red welt swelled up on Teddy's cheek. Even so, the bruises and wounds on Teddy's face and body will never compare to the wounds inflicted on this little boy's heart from the insults hurled at him by his own father. "Don't be a sissy. Be a man! Get out there. Close those barn doors!"

Teddy cried as Daddy dragged him across the bare living room floor toward the swinging doors that opened to the kitchen. Standing off to the side, I scream out, "Please don't hurt my brother! Please don't hurt my brother!"

I heard my mother's pleas, begging Daddy to stop hurting his little boy, which added a softness to this symphony of terror, like a sweet clarinet. When Daddy ignored her, her voice changed to anger. "Ted stop! He's just a little boy. He's afraid."

I ran and threw my body at Daddy's leg and grabbed his pants. As Daddy continued to push Teddy toward the kitchen doors, I held on, sliding across the floor until he shook me off as a puppy pulling on his pants. He kicked his leg and tossed me off to the side. I sat crying and whimpering, still begging, "Please don't hurt my brother."

Daddy was a strong man, full of alcohol he had been drinking all day. He was determined to make a man out of his young boy. Teddy lost the battle. Daddy shoves him through the back door into the stormy night, leaving him alone in the black darkness, with no moon or stars to give him light.

I sat very still, listening to the sobs grow faint as Teddy made his way to the barn doors. The storm overwhelmed his cries. I could no longer hear him. Then the barn doors grew silent; the banging stopped.

Soon I heard Teddy coming through the back door, and I watched him slink back through the swinging doors into the living room. Drenched with the blowing wind and rain, his body shivered. He made his way through the living room, leaving puddles of rainwater behind.

My mother glared her condemnation across the room to Daddy, who's slumped in his favorite chair, holding his whiskey bottle. Mother placed a towel around Teddy's chilled body, comforting him as she led him into the hallway to the bedrooms. I followed.

There was another that weighed in as often. Perhaps it is the one most responsible for my fear of the country night. In pitch black darkness, my older brother, Teddy, four years older, and I, dressed in our pajamas, stood outside, waiting by the door on the front porch.

A naked bulb cast a pale light on my mother's arm sticking out through a crack in the door. She handed us two pillows and disappeared. The door closes, separating her connection to us. Without a word, we knew to wait. Soon her arm reappeared. She handed us a blanket and a Mason jar filled with water.

Holding these necessities for the night, we waited until we saw her thin body squeeze through the cracked door. She eased the door shut behind her, grabbed my hand as we ran to the old car that's waiting in the circular dirt driveway. Teddy ran beside us.

We scrambled into the car, and she closed the door ever so gently. She stuck the key into the ignition. As we listened to the engine grind, our eyes stayed glued on our small house that sits in the middle of a pecan grove. The car lurches forward.

At the main road, we turned right. After a short distance, we made another right turn down a narrow path through the middle of tall corn, its stalk brushing the car windows. The car bounced, threatening to fly apart into small pieces when its bottom scraped the deep ruts left by the plows. We parked the car in the middle of the field. Our mother shuts off the motor and headlights, leaving only the stars and the moon to expose us to the unknown.

In the back seat, Teddy and I each took a pillow and covered up with the blanket. Once again I saw her hand reach toward us, this time, it's an attempt to tuck us in, to give us a feeling of safety and protection. I watched her as she leaned her head back in the front seat behind the wheel, ready to move if necessary.

Crickets rubbed their wings, filling the warm summer air with their mating song. Frogs' throats vibrated their low-pitched voice, and a summer breeze crackled through the tall corn and weeds that surrounded us. A dog sang his lonely song to the moon in the distance. The sounds of the night encompassed us. At another time and place, these sounds might have been a lullaby, but on this night, their eerie sounds reminded us we're all alone.

My small body tightened as I tried to make myself invisible to a monster of my imagination. I couldn't see or describe it, but I knew it was there. I could feel its presence swarming around us, waiting to scoop me into its arms and carry me far away. I was powerless.

The beautiful twinkling lights of the stars served as a measure, magnifying just how far away the monster could take me from my mother. I snuggled closer to my brother, and my hands tightened their grip on our blanket.

This escape to find refuge in a cornfield, or crop of the season in the middle of the night, wasn't our first, nor would it be our last. Still, the fear of the country and the nights we spent hiding in dark fields was minimized only by the fear of losing my mother. That one is a profound fear, visceral and uncontrollable; and it never left me.

Daddy was a binge drinker. Every two weeks he drank non-stop for three or four days, all day, and no sleep for anyone in the house. Just as we settled into a period of peace and sobriety, he walked in, hat cocked, with the kind of grin the kind that signaled my mother to prepare for our escape into the night, knowing that when the dawn breaks we must return and wait again.

While we waited with anticipation, my mother picked her cuticles raw, until they bled.

In the mid-thirties, my parents purchased a farm in Hopkins, South Carolina, a rural area fifteen miles from Columbia where I was born. Hopkins sparsely populated an area dotted by a few landowners, tenant farmers, both black and white, and the hands who worked the fields for small wages. Everyone was suffering from the Great Depression.

Daddy wasn't a farmer. He sold life insurance. He traveled to Columbia to work. I never knew why they bought the farm. It disappointed my mother who had wanted to buy the small house they lived in on Trenholme Road in Columbia, where I was born. Mother worked as a social worker and traveled the county. Both my parents were educated, coming from established, South Carolina families.

How much of these memories happened as I remembered them, I can't tell. When someone mentioned the word fear, my fears of the night, the isolation, the dark, the chaos and the abuse, stir something inside of me that confirms these memories. They were real to me.

But there is more to these memories, too. There is the daytime, the sunshine, butterflies flitting flower to flower. There were birds singing outside the kitchen window, in the tree I climbed. I even remember falling from that tree once. There was a cow with brown spots that swatted its tail at the annoying flies while she stood still for my brother to milk. I remember the buzz of the oversized bumblebees, the fresh smell of the air, and the breezes that come and go on a hot day.

The memory of the bushes, trees, and wildflowers holds a beauty that calms my fears. It reminds me that peace can be found even in the worst fear. Often, as my mother had taught me, I have to "brush it off, Darlin:" and fill my mind with the sunshine, not the dark.

Mary Law Meinelt eats life by the fists full. She is a dedicated writer now in the final stages of writing her memoir as she continues to reinvent herself. She has a BA and MFA in Theater. She is an actor in all unions and paints in her spare time. Her stories are published in Solstice Anthology, The Sun Magazine, The Red Clay Review and Love Alters, which can be purchased on Amazon. She has made finalist in several major contests and is a bronze award winner in a contest for best First Paragraph on Women's Memoir. Mary lives with husband, Carl, her biggest fan, in Durham, N.C.

Fear is faith that something won't work out.
Proverb

Fear Coach

By Niall McInnes

I started out on a journey to make myself harder when I was 20; to toughen me up and be more of a man. I decided that being a man was being courageous. I realized early on that being courageous is different than not being scared. Being courageous was being scared and going anyway.

I got into challenging adrenaline sports: kickboxing, bull riding, bungee jumping, and skydiving. But my real test came with starting a business.

When you ride a bull, you know what you're scared of—you're scared of getting stomped on, crushed, broken and dragged around the arena. When you jump into a ring to fight—you're not scared of getting hurt, you're scared of being beaten up and submitting in front of everyone; showing weakness. So you face the fear and go—it's a rush. It's a primal feeling and the best drug in the world.

The definition is easy. You are in the ring, or you're not. You are on the bull, or you're not. You face the fear and do it, or you don't.

There is no halfway. Starting and running a successful business, though? There is a lot of middle ground.

You can just try it out, you can play it safe, and you can 'dabble.'

When it doesn't work, you will be tempted to blame your upbringing, or your lack of schooling, or the economy. I lied to myself and others for years before I had even begun:

"It won't be that much fun."

"I can't travel."

"I'll be tied down."

But they were just excuses—I was scared.

Scared of failing.
Scared of losing the money I put in,
Scared of being rubbish at my job,
Scared of everyone knowing I'd failed and might think less of me.
I realized this...So I started the business to face my fears.

When you're an entrepreneur—you're not sure what the fear is. Sometimes you just feel lazy or tired—or you think it's just a stupid idea. But it's not. It's FEAR saying that. Fear of getting laughed at, rejected. Fear of failing and everyone finding out. Fear of feeling low because you worked hard and didn't succeed.

Many people play small. Or they never even try.
Their dreams remain dormant and sleepy in their minds.
Their songs left unsung.
FEAR got them,
Because they didn't have someone to say:
"It's okay; it's just fear."
They didn't know that scared feeling in their stomach can be replaced with confidence and excitement.

And that ticks me off.

People can have so much more, and they just don't know how to face the fear.

So now fear IS my business.

My role as a 'Fear Coach' came to mind after holding my very first mindset coaching workshop.

As I was preparing to leave the house, I realized I had the same feeling in my stomach as before a bull ride. I was edgy, panicked, ten things distracting my mind.

There were two factors at play here:

1) The mind cannot distinguish the difference between a real event and a vividly imagined event. I was thinking of the workshop going badly and, as a result, my mind was experiencing the feeling of social rejection.

2) In a nutshell, receptors of physical and emotional pain reside in the same area of the brain.

As a result, my mind was preparing my body with adrenaline to 'escape' the possible pain.

My experience in extreme sports and mindset tools provided me with many ways to combat this—but I realized that most people don't know these tools.

So they just accept the fear.

And when you accept the fear you leave yourself with only two options.

Turn around and quit, or undergo (extreme) stress.

That stress lasts days, weeks or months in the lead up to an event—like the speech at a wedding.

Now, I use my experience from facing fear for many years and my skills as a Master Practitioner of Hypnotherapy, Neuro-Linguistic Programming, and Energy Psychology to help people identify it, know it and remove it from their lives.

I specialize in teaching entrepreneurs how to overcome the fear holding them back.

I show them the best, cutting-edge psychological tools to remove stress and replace it with clarity.

Niall McInnes is a Fear Coach: "I call myself a fear coach. I am a Master Practitioner in Hypnotherapy, Neuro Linguistic Programming, Timeline Transformation and Life Coaching." (niallmcinnes@gmail.com)

Worry gives a small thing a big shadow.
Swedish Proverb

Poetic Pause

Poetry Pebbles

Sometimes poetry is akin to the dress-up fun and purpose of our most formal attire - our Sunday Best. Certainly, good poetry can be full of fancy rhythms, flowing rhyme, and frilly forms, though, poetry is also that great feeling of removing the extra, stuffy, constricting layers. Indeed, poetry is that so anticipated moment of peeling off any stifling materials which encumber us, and replacing them with our minimal "play" clothes to relax and be free.

Connie Kerbs

Life: From Three Best Things....
(Work, Love, and Life)

By Henry Van Dyke (1852-1933)

Let me but live my life from year to year,
With forward face and unreluctant soul;
Not hurrying to, nor turning from the goal;
Not mourning for the things that disappear
In the dim past, nor holding back in fear
From what the future veils; but with a whole
And happy heart, that pays its toll
To Youth and Age, and travels on with cheer.
So let the way wind up the hill or down,
O'er rough or smooth, the journey will be joy:
Still seeking what I sought when but a boy,
New friendship, high adventure, and a crown,
My heart will keep the courage of the quest,
And hope the road's last turn will be the best. (3)

Henry Jackson van Dyke, Jr. (born 1852), a professor of English literature at Princeton for 24 years, was Minister of the Netherlands and Luxembourg in 1913, as WWI broke out. Hellen Keller wrote of him: "Dr. van Dyke is the kind of a friend to have when one is up against a difficult problem. He will take trouble, days and nights of trouble if it is for somebody else..." His poem, "Time Is," was read at the funeral of Diana, Princess of Wales. (4)

Chapter 2

The Hands That Rock The Cradle

Inspired

Children rarely misquote. They typically just repeat word for word what someone shouldn't have said.

Unknown

To our, first, astonishment, and later reflection, we will eventually hear our mother's words coming out of our mouth. Often, it is when we are frustrated or overwhelmed, grasping at our parenting straws. But it is also often when we are in an exceptional parenting moment she would be proud of.

Connie Kerbs

*We were lucky enough to grow up in an environment where there was always much encouragement to children
to pursue intellectual interests;
to investigate whatever aroused curiosity.*

Orville Wright

*The character and history of each child may be a new
and poetic experience to the parent if they will let it.*

Margaret Fuller

Everything depends on upbringing

Leo Tolstoy, War and Peace.

Children are the hands by which we take hold of heaven.

Henry Ward Beecher.

Honey, I Killed Our Kid

By Cory Bartlett

It was a chilly Tuesday morning in November when I looked up from my pancake and asked my wife and son "How's the honey maple syrup?" My wife smiled and remarked with a sound that inferred, "I've died and gone to hot cake heaven." Simultaneously, I remember my sweet little boy, Jackson, nodding his head up and down with a big smile, and a mouth way too full of flapjack. That was the last moment he seemed like himself.

The memory of that day still plays in my head nearly 15 years later. I rewind it from time to time and wonder if I could have changed anything.

Our trip a couple of weeks before the farm and the pumpkin patch resulted in the acquisition of three festive treats: 1) Honey 2) Maple Honey Syrup and 3) Pumpkins for Jack-O-Lanterns. With only a few days to go before Halloween, we scrambled to make the most out of our harvested items.

Pumpkins were carved expediently into a cat, a clown, and a ghost and placed on the porch with care. The honey-sweetened sandwiches, ham, and breakfast oatmeal. Halloween came and went, and the honey maple syrup sat in the cupboard, still sealed farm fresh, until Veteran's Day.

My office near downtown closed that Veteran's Day as it was only a few weeks since the tragic events of 9/11 in New York. We lived only a mile away from my office and close to downtown shopping. I was in advertising then, and for those who remember even that Christmas of 2001 was a somber one.

I figured I'd make the most of a morning at home and wake up my wife and son by cooking my usual Sunday morning brunch with omelets and some fried potatoes. To my delight, I discovered the all-natural, Maple Honey syrup in the cupboard! It was then I decided to throw together some *panny's* on the griddle. (Yes, I call them *panny's* sometimes.)

After breakfast, Jackson stood up from the table. He looked a little queasy. I asked him if he was alright, and he said, "Yeah." Then he sauntered off like he had eaten a little too much. He had cleaned his plate, unusual for him, but I figured he must have loved the pancakes.

After cleaning up the kitchen, I went into the living room and sat down on the couch. Veteran's Day ceremonies from around the nation displayed on the morning news breaks. Flags were still in high prominence from that September. I changed channels when I heard a groan coming from his bedroom. I went to his room and said, "You okay bud?" He looked pale. He had a fever. I went to the bathroom and found some ibuprofen and gave him half a tablet. He swallowed it and then laid down on his bed. I went back to the television and watched "The Price is Right" for a few minutes.

Suddenly, I heard crying coming from his room. I got up to see what was going on. As I opened his door, I noticed he was fussing and rolling around on his bed like he couldn't quite reach what was bothering him on his back. I went in and said, "Are you itchy?" He nodded yes. I lifted up his shirt and saw dozens of small red blotches and bumps on his back. I looked at his chest; it was clear. His fever was getting worse, so I walked him in to see his Mom. "Honey, look at Jackson. He doesn't feel too well." Melody looked at him and said, "Maybe he just needs to lay down for a little." I agreed. It was then I told him we were going to take off his shirt and pants and put on jammies. He said, "Daddy I'm itching really bad." When I took off his shirt, I noticed the red dots had spread to his chest and stomach. Hundreds of them in a matter of a few seconds. I told Melody to call Dr. Kincaid and made the instant decision to run him downtown to his pediatrician's office.

As we got in the car, I noticed his condition had worsened. Now, the redness had started to creep into his cheeks and forehead. I realized he must be having an allergic reaction.

As we pulled into the doctor's office about two blocks away from the hospital, I noticed he was fully red and flushed in the face and neck. The dots had merged into one giant blotch all over his skin on his chest, neck, and back. I hurriedly carried him out of the car into the doctor's office. The receptionist told us, "The Doctor will be right with you." We sat down as Jackson's breathing seemed fast and unproductive. I was on the verge of telling the receptionist when we were called back.

Miraculously, Dr. Kincaid came into the room almost immediately. Jackson's eyes had started looking droopy, and he began to lose consciousness. I knew we had to help him right then. Dr. Kincaid entered the room and said, "Oh my. We've got to get him over to the hospital right now!" He said, "Pick up your boy and follow me." I scooped Jackson up in my arms and realized he had lost his bowels in his pants. I told the doctor, "He pooped his pants." Dr. Kincaid said, "Mr. Bartlett, we need to run."

At that instant, my son lost consciousness. My heart was racing. I could feel my little boy's heart pounding, and I felt his breathing as it changed to a labored quick and panting kind. We exited the office and ran across the parking lot towards the hospital entrance. Dr. Kincaid led the way, and I was in a solid jog. When we had to pause for traffic, Dr. Kincaid asked, "Is he still breathing?" I listened for a moment, amidst all the sounds of a busy city's downtown area, and watched his chest rise and fall. "Yes," I replied. The "Don't Walk" red light was flashing, and Dr. Kincaid ran into the crosswalk stopping traffic, I ran behind him and then in front of him toward the emergency room entrance of the hospital. He wouldn't catch up to me until I went inside the doors.

Immediately, I cried out "Help! My son needs help!" and the emergency room staff came running. They ushered me through a door into an emergency operating room, and I laid Jackson's lifeless little body down on the white-sheeted bed. Tears were streaming down my face. I no longer saw his chest rise and fall. He had stopped breathing. Dr. Kincaid ran into the room and said, "Adrenaline! This boy is having an allergic reaction!" The nurses scrambled for the medication, and I stood there helpless watching as they hooked up my little boy to machines. I heard one nurse say, "Pulse is faint." I felt myself start to hyperventilate. Another nurse said, "Sir, it may be better if you leave the room." I said "No ma'am. I'm not leaving his side." I went in close to my son, to hold his little hand. His fever seemed to be gone. He felt almost cold.

The drawn curtain suddenly pulled back, as Dr. Kincaid emerged with a large, hypodermic needle. Without hesitation, he plunged the needle deep into Jackson's sternum and injected the adrenaline. He pulled the needle out, as my heart sank. I said to myself, "God, please let my boy live."

I began to flash back to when he was a little boy, changing his diapers, helping him toddle and walk. I remembered looking into his eyes for the first time as my wife gave birth to him a month earlier than we had expected. His beautiful brown eyes he had received from me.

My brown eyes were closed when I heard his gasp. I opened my eyes and saw him sit straight up in the bed as nurses tried to keep him calm and hold him down. He was alive! His eyes opened. He was breathing! Almost immediately I could see the red begin to disappear from his skin and be replaced by his natural tone. He was jittery and shaking a little. His system was in a full state of shock. I wanted to hold him and hug him, but the medical team was still working on him in front of me, so I just hit my knees and cried. Dr. Kincaid put his hand on me and said, "He's going to be okay, Cory." I placed my hand on his and said, "Thank you, thank you so much, doctor." After a minute or two, I started to compose myself and stood up.

After a few more minutes of getting Jackson hooked up to an I.V. and checking vitals, the medical team cleared some, and I approached him. His eyes were still wide open, and I placed my hand on his forehead gently brushing his hair back. "Hey buddy," I said. He looked over at me and muttered, "Hey."

I said, "You're going to be okay, honey." He said, "Good," and nodded a little. I smiled the purest of smiles. I knew we had felt the touch of God's hand that day. I knew my little boy had just barely survived by His grace.

A few weeks later we were undergoing allergy testing and discovered he had slight reactions to both honey and the medicinal family of macrolides. This family of medicines is the same as that of Motrin and Ibuprofen. We later learned that all-natural honey could contain a stronger type of unfiltered honey which may include pollens from multiple natural wildflowers. A perfect storm likely happened when it combined in his system with the ibuprofen I gave him for his fever.

Today, Jackson is 17 years old and is a senior in the high school where I teach. He plays baseball, loves video games like every other teenager these days, and recently attended Homecoming with his girlfriend. He worked part-time at McDonald's for a year after turning 16 and getting his license and currently is employed by Best Western Hotels. He takes his SAT exam in a month and is in the process of applying for admission to a college where he plans to follow in my footsteps and pu9333rsue a career in teaching. He has two little sisters, Madison age 9 and Alison age 6—neither of whom have allergies.

Cory Bartlett has almost 14 years of teaching and administrative experience as a Technology, Business, and Marketing instructor. He has served as an officer in numerous community organizations, state education boards, and associations. He holds a Master's Degree in Education and will graduate in 2016 with his Doctorate in Educational Administration. He resides in Ritzville, Washington with his wife of 19 years and their three children.

You think I'm licked. You all think I'm licked. Well, I'm not licked! And I'm going to stay right here and fight for this lost cause! Even if the room gets filled with lies...and the...armies come marching into this place...

(James Stewart as Jefferson Smith in Mr. Smith Goes to Washington)

What is Fear?

By Lainie Liberti

As clear as I recalled my breakfast just a few hours ago, I can recall a most severe encounter with fear that took place over fourteen years ago. Miro was a new-born, just a few months old. I can recall how sweet he smelled, how soft his skin felt and how much love warmed my soul each time I looked into my tiny baby's eyes. I can still hear his sweet giggle and see his eyes light up in my mind's eye as if it was happening at this moment.

Miro and I had received an invitation from one of the parents from our birthing class. It was an invitation to meet other families we knew before their children's birth. I was excited to see everyone and meet their babies. On the evening of our get-together, I became terrified of driving, experiencing irrational fears wash over me.

"Don't go; you'll crash your car. Don't go; you'll die, you'll get lost and be violently killed, mutilated, decapitated. Don't go; your child will be kidnapped, taken from you, sold on the black market. Don't go, you'll die in a horrible explosion, and you and your precious baby will burn to a cinder. Don't go; your child will be in a horrible accident. Don't go; you'll ruin Miro's entire life. Don't go. Something terrible is going to happen to you both. Don't go," the voice of fear shouted over and over in my head.

I could not quiet my voice of fear no matter how hard I tried. Instead, I tried to reason with the voice of fear shouting louder and louder in my head.

"It isn't that far to drive; I drove much farther to work on a daily basis for years and years. It wasn't rush-hour, and I know the freeways well," I pleaded with the voice.

It was straight up I-5 to 134, a clear shot from downtown Los Angeles to the Valley. I knew the route. I told myself it was irrational and I tried to ignore the voice. The more I tried to ignore it, the more it demanded my attention, yelling louder, insisting I listen.

It said, "You never have thoughts like this, so listen now." Louder and LOUDER the fearful voice became, and the more I resisted it, the louder the voice shouted at me. I managed to arrive at the party on time and had a semi-lovely visit with all the new families. But frequently, that voice in my head started up again. I became increasingly nervous about the drive home.

I dreaded leaving because, at that point, one fearful thought led to another more fearful thought. Five minutes into my drive home on the empty Los Angeles Freeway, I was forced to pull off onto the shoulder. I sobbed, frozen in fear. I was scared. No, I was terrified. Not just terrified, but petrified. I froze with fear and could not move. I wasn't sure of exactly what, but I looked over at my beautiful newborn son fast asleep in his car seat, and I sobbed on the side of the freeway because I was too afraid to drive. It took me close to an hour to gain my composure enough to attempt driving again.

It was an irrational fear, but it controlled me; completely. I could not do anything to combat it, and the cascading thoughts, one on top of another turned into a snowball of fear, freezing me from taking any action. I could only sit there, on the side of the freeway, and cry while shaking.

Fortunately, that is the most severe bout I've had with fear. This reminder of the power of fear, that completely out-of-control fear, the kind that managed to control me spooked me more than ever now. Who was the voice of this fear? Why did it have so much power in my head? Before our travels, my relationship to fear was completely unconscious. When it did rear its ugly head, I was acutely aware of its presence.

I knew intimately the physical responses fear caused in my body from the racing heart, sweaty palms, to the dry mouth and the freezing in action. However, I never considered my relationship to fear anything but "normal" as many I knew experienced panic attacks and crippling anxiety.

And that certainly wasn't me.

A friend on Facebook said this about the difference between fear and anxiety:

"I see a spider: Fear.

A spider is on me: Panic and Anxiety."

Many of my friends have had panic attacks and anxiety disorders, but that did not happen to me. I was certain I had a "normal" relationship to fear, and that my fear was neither overreaching, nor absent, and my fears were "respectable."

On the few occasions when my fear managed to dominate my experience, I acquiesced to its power and just let it run its course, without question. After all, what choice did I have? We all know, "fear "is bigger than the individual and there is absolutely nothing a person could do about it. Right?

Fear must have been designed to keep us safe on some level, activating the fight or flight reaction. But somewhere down the line, the purpose of fear in our lives was usurped and used to manipulate us. Advertising, governments, religions all used fear as a means to control the masses.

Fears are real. But what of our personal fears? What of those emotionally controlling thoughts which we label personal fears? Those are shame-filled, meant to be kept quiet and hidden.

Mix 2 parts fear, 1 part shame; shake until dissolved. If fear does not dissolve, cover in an airtight container. mix with medication, (prescription or self-medicating), your choice. In all cases, you must do whatever you can do to ACT NORMAL!

Within American culture, fear plays a major role. However on a personal level, fear may be a person's greatest teacher. In many respects for Miro and I, fear helped us transform our lives.

Understanding Fear and My Own Fearful Thoughts

In the early days of our travels, again, fear washed over me. I felt on edge, wide-eyed and timid. I remember stepping into the hot Mexico air, feeling disoriented, confused and completely out of my comfort zone. I felt afraid that I had made a terrible mistake. I felt the fear that Miro and I were in danger. I felt certain something terrible would happen to us. I had so many fearful thoughts taking over my head I felt, once again, like that new mother stuck on the side of the freeway frozen in fear. I was afraid, and full-blown fear dominated my experience.

I realized very quickly fear had no place to hide. Fear was either going to control our travels or become a quiet companion. I committed to the later.

Even though I was feeling full-blown fear during the first days of our travels, I had a sense that my fears were irrational. The idea of having "irrational thoughts" led me to the belief that my fears were indeed nothing more than "thoughts." I had promised myself that under no circumstances could I allow Miro to see the fear I was experiencing, nor would I allow him to take on my fears as his own. The more I became clear of my commitment to travel without fear, the more I became obsessed with not allowing fear to control my experience. Nor Miro's.

As I made the connection that my overwhelming fears were just a series of, "fearful thoughts," a light bulb went off. Thoughts! Hmmm... I had some experience dealing with, "limiting beliefs," during my quest for self-healing childhood issues. I read dozens of self-help books, practiced meditations and explored multiple healing modalities.

But this was the first time I treated my fears as thoughts, instead of a powerful monster that could rule my life. "Thoughts." I had dealt with them in the past and found Byron Katie's, The Work, helpful in challenging limiting beliefs. I bet the same process would work on "fear," too as I was adamant to view fears as nothing more than powerful thoughts.

That became the turning point in dissolving my fears.

My Relationship to Fear NOW

As Miro and I moved through our first year of travels together, we continued to talk about fear, intuition, and inspiration quite a bit. We practiced focusing our attention on those feelings as tools instead of giving the power to fear. Only then, when we brought a conscious intention to the fear we now call, "fearful thoughts," we discovered that we were stronger than them.

Realizing, "there is nothing to fear," liberated our travels, freeing us to become more adventurous.

Now, I realize that fear is a trick my brain used to keep me focused on thoughts that were "future" based. Keeping focused on the future ultimately prevented us from venturing out of our comfort zone in the present. (Focusing on the future is just as dangerous as focusing on the past. It is kind of like a dog chasing its tail for hours upon end.)

We generally feel safe in the world. That is not to say life never presents us with scary situations. But when it does, our instinct kicks in. As was the case on that I had to pick up a rock to defend myself. But now, I refer to it as instinct.

Now, without fear, Miro and I became freer in the present moment, and inspiration became our guide. Years into our travels, my son and I have learned these lessons, and continue to deepen our relationship with the world because of these amazing tools we've found within ourselves.

Lainie Liberti dedicates her energies to the alternative education movement and together with her son Miro, slow travel around the globe, living an inspired possession-free-lifestyle, volunteering and learning naturally (www.raisingmiro.com). She produces a series of teen-oriented retreats called Project World School and has hosted a popular internet show on the Conscious Consumer Network called For the Love of Learning, Voices of the Alternative Education Movement.

Nothing is so much to be feared as fear.
Henry David Thoreau,

Poetic Pause

Poetry Pebbles

A poet is a nightingale, who sits in darkness and sings to cheer its own solitude with sweet sounds.

Percy Bysshe Shelley

Turn to poetry to help deal with the flow of magma that bubbles below an explosive outpouring of powerful things pent up deep and long- not too unlike a volcano. Vent the vast reservoir of pressurized material, and you just might save yourself — and
everyone else for miles around. At the very least, this will lessen
the vigor of such an eminently destructive eruption. The worst this can do is nothing, but it just might ease the pressure and channel at least some of the energy out in a more controlled fashion. This method also allows for a safely distanced, keen observation of such awesome forces.

Connie Kerbs

The Sick Child

By: Robert Louis Stevenson

CHILD.
O Mother, lay your hand on my brow!
O mother, mother, where am I now?
Why is the room so gaunt and great?
Why am I lying awake so late?
MOTHER.
Fear not at all: the night is still.
Nothing is here that means you ill -
Nothing but lamps the whole town through,
And never a child awake but you.
CHILD.
Mother, mother, speak low in my ear,
Some of the things are so great and near,
Some are so small and far away,
I have a fear that I cannot say,
What have I done, and what do I fear,
And why are you crying, mother dear?
MOTHER.
Out in the city, sounds begin
Thank the kind God, the carts come in!
An hour or two more, and God is so kind,
The day shall be blue in the window-blind,
Then shall my child go sweetly asleep,
And dream of the birds and the hills of sheep. (5)

Robert Louis Stevenson's boyhood was influenced by a grandfather, a minister and philosopher, who shared his love of sermons and storytelling with his tenderhearted, receptive grandson. Throughout his childhood, he was prone to illness, and often bedridden. During these bouts, he devoured the likes of Shakespeare and Bunyon, among others of the era, all which helped nurture a love of great literature. Despite his passions leading his heart and mind elsewhere, insubstantial, commendable efforts to please his father's desires that he should pursue a career in law, he passed the bar at 25. As most recognize, he is the author of Treasure Island, The Strange Case of Dr. Jekyll and Mr. Hyde, and A Child's Garden of Verse. Stevenson is one of the most well known and beloved authors of the world, and is the 25th most translated author of his era, surpassing many other well known and beloved others of the era. (6)

Oh, fear not in a world like this,
And thou shalt know ere long—
Know how sublime a thing it is
To suffer and be strong.

Henry Wadsworth Longfellow

Chapter 3

Speaking Of

Inspired

Let us never fear robbers or murderers.
They are dangers from without, petty dangers.
Let us fear ourselves.
Prejudices are the real robbers;
Vices are the real murderers.
The great dangers lie within ourselves.
What matters it if something threatens our head or our purse!
Let us think only of that which threatens the soul.

Victor Hugo

Time is so difficult to comprehend really, and it gets away from all of us just in the few decades we have here. If we're honest, for most of us at least, even with the benefit of faith and hope and all that these mean to us, for the time-being in this existence, the afterlife is just impossible for us to grasp. No matter, in the end—
because eternity is still just a really, really, very long time.
Perhaps one of the most important things
to do is focus on having a better sense of
humor before we get there...before we are all together...
for eternity.
Which could be a considerably long time, after all.

Connie Kerbs

I may be compelled to face danger, but never fear it, and while our soldiers can stand and fight, I can stand and feed and nurse them.

Clara Barton

Clarity

By Jonty Bush

Growing up, I had always presumed that we received a sign before the occurrence of a life-changing event. A lightning bolt perhaps, or an ominous storm, but the day my life changed started like any other. It was, in fact, a beautiful day, the day I learned my sister and father had been murdered. I say this in one sentence, but in fact, they were two separate incidents, just four months apart and in separate, unrelated circumstances.

When something terrible happens, life becomes complicated. You're thrown into a world of new language and jargon—suddenly my life was filled with judicial terms like *committal, evidence, mens-rea*, and *beyond a reasonable doubt*. I was arranging two funerals, managing wills, estates, family court orders… all while trying to live and grieve.

Life becomes complicated, and yet, in ways, life becomes simpler too. Adversity is like a sieve in which all of life's events pour into. As we shake and sift this apparatus of life, the things that are no longer important fall through and all that is left behind are the things that matter; suddenly exposed and clear.

I was surprised at the clarity I experienced in the aftermath of homicide. People ask me how I survived the grief and shock of losing loved ones to murder, and for many years, I would shrug and mumble things about 'getting on with it.' I felt I should be saying something more insightful, but as I matured in confidence, I realized simply it's just a matter of getting on.

Of course, just because it's simple, that doesn't mean it's easy. For years, I carried an internal battle between my heart that wanted to move on, wanted to forgive… and my head who would argue that

I *should* be upset, that I *shouldn't* be happy, that I *should* be angry and seek justice and fight.

This was my first real experience of fear. A fear of being judged. Fear that people thought I didn't love my family enough. It takes incredible strength and courage to challenge the labels society wants to place on us. When a person is thrown into a system that disempowers, it triggers a fear reaction from us. It is that reaction where our impulse is to control, fight and win. The true key to our strength lies in not succumbing to the game.

It requires us to search deeply within ourselves and discover what our own truth is. What our needs are (not what they should be), what our hopes are (no matter how much they frighten us), and what we value (regardless of whether it fits with others' expectations). Adversity helps us do this. Tough times are incredibly revealing: I learned more about myself in the first year after the homicides, than I had in the twenty-one years preceding it.

The key, in my opinion, is to ask yourself, *How do I want to be telling this story in ten years?* Do you want to be the victim or the hero of the narrative? Becoming the hero takes work from day one? Don't wait until you're feeling courageous enough to tackle life's big issues; that time will never come. Courage comes through facing our fears.

Jonty Bush is a resilience coach, speaker, and writer with the experience of what it takes to channel adversity into action. Following the homicides of her sister and father, Jonty commenced a career working with victims of violence. She has successfully lobbied parliament for legislative improvements for victims of crime and established the National One Punch Can Kill anti-violence campaign. Jonty lives and works in Australia, she is a mother of four (including three stepchildren), and continues to work with the Department of Justice. You can connect with Jonty at www.jontybush.com.au.

It is never too late to be what you might have been.
George Eliot

The Fear Phenomenon

By Roxanie Lebsanft

Studies of the world's great entrepreneurs and leaders have discovered that they share something termed 'productive paranoia.'

They are great at predicting worst-case scenarios and being the devil's advocate. They'll even ask others for their opinion on everything that could go wrong to make sure they've covered every base in their planning for success.

Leaders catastrophize to decrease stress, but not everyone experiences it as comforting. Most find catastrophizing stressful, to the point of overwhelming, yet it happens frequently.

What is the difference between healthy and unhealthy fear?

Feeling helpless or empowered can depend on how we manage to catastrophize, i.e., *worry wart syndrome*. The differences lie in the 'fact-finding' process.

Feeling helpless and fearful about, "What if…?" comes from a lack of evidence gathering. This future imagining of what could happen is often devoid of probability or fact. People regularly overestimate how accurate their predictive abilities are, often basing their assumptions on past experiences, which are no longer relevant or real.

How often have you experienced imagining how something will play out, rolling it around in your mind over and over again and then found the event has happened, and it was nothing like you thought it would be? Usually, it's much simpler, less dramatic and often anticlimactic. People will regularly say, "I don't know what all the worrying was about! What a waste of energy!"

Also, the more horrifying a prediction imagined is, the more engrossed the mind becomes and the more it believes in the imagined scenario. For example, someone terrified of spiders will over-actively imagine dying a horrible death from even the tiniest spider, yet not look after their health to prevent a much more predictable and likely chronic illness. Imagination gravitates to the most gruesome, devastating, fearful outcomes, not the most likely.

This very reason explains why the most successful and popular suspense novels and dramatic thrillers are often graphic; because they play into our need for extremes to engage the imagination.

Leaders know this and, therefore, don't panic or feel overwhelmed.

They allow imagination to inform them of their fears, but they also know how to ignore the dramatics and instead focus on the most likely risks, working to reduce those. How can we learn from them?

How about becoming more scientific, like Sherlock Holmes?

If you or someone you know is overwhelmed with anxiety or fear, it's time to look at the most likely, predictable outcomes.

Based on what you know; strengths, weaknesses, resources and past experiences, how likely is the most feared outcome? If the worst-case scenario were to come true, how could you put protective buffers into action now to prevent it from happening?

Fact-finding is the best fear annihilator. Questions like, "What's happening right now?" and, "Is this reality-based or likely?" help to reign in imagination, and allows for the rational part of the mind to engage.

Experts also know the fight/flight response is triggered 100,000 times faster than the rational part of our brain. It takes a minimum of seven seconds for the mind to catch up and think rationally about a situation. Taking seven long breaths before jumping to fearful conclusions can offer the means to deal with reality more thoughtfully.

Base fears on well-founded research and predictable outcomes as well as imagination. Being overwhelmed decreases, and positive actions are likely to result in long-term, sustainable, healthy habits of both mind and body. Imagination—make it a friend, not a foe.

Roxanie Lebsanft is a psychotherapist and lecturer in psychotherapy, founder of Bare Hands, which is a company that provides emotional intelligence education for resilience, aimed at women dealing with stress. She has been a successful clinical practitioner for over 13 years.
(www.barehands.com.au), Resilience for Women

Fear is the mother of foresight.
Thomas Hardy

Poetic Pause

Poetry Pebbles

Poetry is a powerful, pouring river flowing out of our greatest joys. It is also that waterfall of tears that gushes forth, out of our most intense grief.

Connie Kerbs

Poetry surrounds us everywhere, but putting it on paper is, alas, not so easy as looking at it.

Vincent Van Gogh

Fear in Facets

By Cesar Moran-Cahusac

Fear is a furious charge of dark black fury
Of a beast with a hate-gaze and nostrils with acrid fumes
One that lowers it horns solely to thrust and pierce dreams
Nothing stops the forceful obliteration of this raging Miura bull
Anything that dares to make the bold move of keeping one's
Magic in place,

To show off bare skin of the tattooed attitude alive…
Will get trampled, torn to bits and pieces
Yes, fear is the fiend with a hate-gaze,
It's the spirit that hovers over us to decimate, to kill will.

So to dismantle its strength, look at its eyes.
And as it tells us: Mind the gap, to feed us with illusory danger
Engage it by behaving as a daring bumble bee bouncing around
Inconceivably flying, disregarding the assertion of caution.

In this way, it shall never become your glossy shield.
That covers all like morning frost drying up the leaves it embraces
Fear is the fractal fairyland of false security,
It has no cohesion if one faces it with vitality

Show your bare skin *peeling resistance present your vulnerability
And just like that, the monstrous sand statue with saber horns
Will collapse corroded by your ocean breeze.

Cesar Moran-Cahusac's poetry weaves an expansive range of exotic, sensual and surprising life experiences into a dance of verbal refinement. He is the author of the book of popular poetry entitled: "She Said No to the Wind."

I by no means rank poetry high in the scale of intelligence—this may look like affectation—but it is my real opinion—it is the lava of the imagination; whose eruption prevents an earthquake.

Lord Byron, letter to Annabella Milbanke (29 November 1813)

Chapter 4

Nuts and Bolts

Inspired

So, first of all, let me assert my firm belief that the only thing we have to fear is…fear itself. Nameless, unreasoning, unjustified terror which paralyzes needed efforts to convert retreat into advance.

Franklin D. Roosevelt, First Inaugural Address, 1933

Nothing in life is to be feared; it is only to be understood. Now is the time to understand more, so that we may fear less.

Marie Curie

*Start a huge, foolish project like Noah.
It makes absolutely no difference what people think of you.*

Rumi

Do not be too timid and squeamish about your actions. All life is an experiment. The more experiments you make, the better.

Ralph Waldo Emerson (1842)

*Never let fear determine how you see yourself;
And never let your past determine your future.*

Connie Kerbs

Fight, Flight or Freeze

By Connie Kerbs

Almost everyone is familiar with the fight-flight response—your reaction to a stimulus perceived as an imminent threat to your survival. Less well-known is the fight-flight-freeze response, which adds a crucial dimension to how you react when the situation at hand overwhelms your coping and leaves you paralyzed in fear. (7).

Here, in brief, is how the survival-oriented acute stress response operates. Accurately or not, if you assess the immediately menacing force as something you potentially have the power to defeat, you go into fight mode. In such instances, the hormones released by your sympathetic nervous system—especially adrenaline—prime you to do battle and, hopefully, triumph over the hostile entity.

Conversely, if you view the antagonistic force as too powerful to overcome, your impulse is to outrun it (and the faster, the better). This, of course, is the flight response, also linked to the instantaneous ramping up of your emergency biochemical supplies—so that, ideally, you can escape from this perceived adversarial power (whether it be human, animal, or some calamity of nature).

So where does the totally disabling freeze response fit? By default, this reaction refers to a situation in which you've concluded (in a matter of seconds—if not milliseconds) that you can neither defeat the frighteningly dangerous opponent confronting you nor safely bolt from it. Ironically, this self-paralyzing response can at the moment be just as adaptive as either valiantly fighting the enemy or, more cautiously, fleeing from it.

Consider situations in which there really is no way you can defend yourself. You have neither the adrenaline-assisted strength to respond aggressively to the hostile force nor the anxiety-driven speed to free yourself from it. You feel utterly helpless: neither fight nor flight is viable, and there's no one on the scene to rescue you.

Or, consider those situations that are more intellectual or emotional, or social in threat than physical. Fitting this bill would be life's difficult circumstances requiring consideration time of all the important decisions at hand. These times include the likes of sudden job loss, domestic betrayal, abandonment or divorce, serious health problems, or other troubling financial or emotional stress.

There are at least two main schools of thought on the freeze in our fear: one is that the freeze is actually just a pause to slow down an unhelpful reaction, overreaction, or unnecessary response to any given situation. It is a gift of time to think through the threat and come up with the most rational, effective response to the situation at hand. The other, long-standing definition of the "freeze," mode of our fear, is that it is a kind of "numbing out," or disassociation in terror-laden circumstances that have overcome us, besieging us with trepidation, immobilizing us with what is actually a hyperaroused state. Both theories are right. And there is more.

There are circumstances where "freezing," is the best (only) option, as escape is hopeless for the time being, and fighting would be futile. Science would say "flying under the radar," is a proven defense mechanism, and does work in some cases of imminent harm. Sometimes doing nothing, in a holding pattern of ultimate stillness will allow the danger just to pass over. Just ask the opossum. Or the mouse who plays dead, declining to trigger the cat's instincts to attack—until the cat gets distracted or loses interest, creating a window of possible escape for the would-be feline's entertaining snack.

Also, it has been discovered that in some such circumstances, some of the chemicals produced, endorphins, etc., in "the freeze," have analgesic properties that would minimize the immediate pain of injury, (psychological or physical). Some more harrowing circumstances are also less likely to be fully experienced as a result of this altered state of consciousness. Thus the imprinting of a detailed memory (if even remembered at all), is stifled as the chemicals involved that immobilize a person in this condition—also arrest the full cognitive processing or taking in of what is happening in "real time."

People experiencing this have described a sense of lost time or feeling *surreal*. Others explain a kind of *out-of-body experience* during this acute kind of fear-stress.

This author's personal (experientially only qualified) opinion is that these circumstances are events that do occur. I am also confident science doesn't fully understand it yet, and how the nuances of this "freeze," play out, physiologically in our experiences. It's not hard to see what is described here, when you read some of the stories in this book or when one thinks about events in one's own plethora of experience where this "freeze," has occurred. Think of the car wreck you don't remember, the wedding or graduation day jitters that induce a kind of *social* amnesia making the special day an event to remember only "in hazy pieces," for many graduates, brides, and grooms, and sometimes their parents. Childbirth is another opportunity to experience this memory lag for many parents, whether the epidural or natural childbirth were experienced- and for the father sometimes, almost as much as the mother. (As much or more in some cases of paternal stress reactions!)

It's been noted the freeze response occurs more in children than adults. Some have speculated this to be because of the child's increased (in sheer numbers) experiences of overwhelming fear, just due to their size and vulnerability. Some children are so sensitive that even a cross look from a parent can invoke strong feelings of rejection and abandonment.

Such times are so painful, a child's unconscious mind may invoke the "check-out," option to get through such anguish. As a person matures, these circumstances are more infrequent. And they are far less ominous when they occur and are (hopefully) experienced from a more reality-based perspective; one that doesn't lay them out with vulnerability and extreme stress every time they experience corrective criticism or furrowed brows.

Some have hypothesized that various psychological phenomena that involve "paralyzing fear," like some OCD's, panic attacks, phobias, and other anxieties may be unresolved "freeze," events that left the person somewhat "stuck," in the original experience of extreme fear. Post-traumatic stress disorder (PTSD) and some of its variants, often tie back to unresolved trauma experiences.

This is also when, what may have been a blessing, or great help in coping with extreme stress as a child can become destructive and maladaptive in our adulthood—sometimes referred to as "toxic."

Ironically, this type of "freezing," (a "numbing," state of dissociation) isn't helpful or life-preserving at all. In fact, it could be very dangerous, preventing a positive, common-sense response to a real or perceived danger; instead, triggering a stymied, *in*appropriate reaction based on irrational fears, or exaggerated emotional responses. This doesn't help to deal with any real problems—especially truly ominous ones. And it may create a chronic false alarm scenario—which is just as ineffective and disruptive in one's life. Just ask the boy who cried wolf, or the executive whose career is thwarted due to their fear of flying.

Psychological premises have proposed that dissociating in the midst of a traumatic experience is the strongest indicator of PTSD symptoms developing later on (see, e.g., van der Kolk & van der Hart, 1989). As mentioned above, children who are already predisposed to dissociate during stressful events of domestic abuse or traumatic episodes, are more vulnerable to a dis-associative response (a paralyzing freeze) later on. Sometimes this is brought on unexpectedly or by unrelated, or even non-specific triggers.

Sometimes, something unexpected will induce unconscious memories of the acute anxiety linked to the original trauma experienced as a child.

An example would be a child who grew up with parents who constantly fought, leading to intensely scary, disruptive, even violent experiences.

Later, when these adult children have an argument with a friend, spouse or another family member, they may have a tendency to shut down or have difficulty with normal conflict. They might struggle poignantly to find healthy resolutions for even minor, such ordeals in their life.

They may be truly unable to work through to the other side of the argument effectively. They may do anything to avoid conflict, including resorting to unhealthy, or maladaptive ways of dealing with *normal* disagreements. They may suddenly, with no explanation, avoid or cut off honest communication, even intimacy—all in the interest of avoiding the fear-inducing struggles that trigger their old emotions of overwhelming trauma.

Of course, this type of emotional response, withdrawal, and lack of effective communication is difficult to maintain in a relationship and will lead to disappointment, isolation, and frustration for both individuals in the partnership. Unresolved problems may even lead to deep, emotional, and finally, actual separation of the couple.

These circumstances, or any of their kin, are candidates for professional support to finally work through these issues that will just go on interfering with normalcy and fulfillment in one's life if not finally confronted. It's important to finally settle any left-over angst, or unresolved past issues involving emotional, physical or psychological trauma. There are many options available for dealing with these issues now, and finally releasing residual tension left from a traumatic event, whenever it may have been experienced.

Resolving toxic *baggage* can also be done by dispelling negative energy from past trauma that manifests itself in the body as stress-related disease or chronic physiological problems. There is significant evidence correlating chronic stress or debilitating, unresolved psycho-emotional trauma with physiological illness.

There is much and ever-mounting evidence connecting the manifesting of such physical symptoms directly to psychological factors. That is not to say that illness is necessarily psychologically induced; however, overall well-being certainly plays a role in how our body handles disease and environmental stress, like viral or infectious exposures. Some studies indicate that stress affects the immune system, whose job is to ward off foreign invasion as much as manage cell deformity and stave off internal threats of cellular and chemical degradation.

There are countless postulates and studies that offer explanations on the mind-body connection, as it relates to stress and illness. A significant volume of research has scientifically demonstrated tangent connections that make up a complex physiology that responds markedly better to scientifically based, holistic approaches to healing. Everything from chemical depression stemming from suppressed fear, to stress-inducing chemical addictions of all kinds, even the obesity-diabetes link, to major illness triggered by negative "life events," such as the death of a spouse or an unwanted divorce.

One of the things we know for sure is that we have far to go to fully understand the individually unique response system that puts our fear *on ice*. We also have much to explore about the resources to deal with it, when it finally, unexpectedly, *thaws out*.

Or was that our (unconscious) plan all along? To save something too difficult and overwhelming for our current resources to deal with until we could more effectively overcome? Some even qualify this experience to be one of the *spiritual realms*. Perhaps rightfully so, this falls into that widely considered and most intensely curious topic of the ages—the mind, body, spirit connection.

Basic happiness is almost entirely dependent on our internal condition—our deep, inside perspective of a typically flawed external.
We will simply never have enough, be enough, do enough, or know enough to achieve anything but fleeting, elusive thrills based on a false confidence in the highly unstable fabric of our current existence. Any enduring happiness is found in the blend of toleration, calm acceptance, and a continued brightness of hope for improvement in the imperfect things in our life.

Any sense of basic happiness stems from a deep, internalized and driving belief in the eventual positive resolution to our struggles.
It's all about what's in order on the inside.
It's all about our capacity for compassion, and ability to muster a smile of gratitude and courage - no matter what fear we face,
no matter the trouble that may surround us.

Connie Kerbs

Dying to Fly

By Ray Wood

Always believe that God is with you, and fear nothing.
Amelia Earhart

The fear of flying is a common condition that often paralyzes a large number of travelers. Air transport is, after all, to embark on a huge winged tube flying at high speeds thousands of feet above solid ground. This fear can become a real ordeal for many people and even simply prevent them from going abroad.

The airplane is now a very common means of transportation, even essential at some point. Whether for holidays or business, the number of people who are afraid of flying is impressive, and the reported fears are very diverse, ranging from simple stress to palpitations, through claustrophobia or crisis panic.

The fear of flying is nothing exceptional. Thirty percent of people have a fear of flying to one degree or another. It takes many different forms. Some people manage to convince themselves of flying but suffer from stress. Others are limited by taking airplanes less frequently and feel intense anxiety during the whole flight. Finally, there are those who do not take planes at all, which often causes them issues in their private lives or complicates their professional life.

People who fear flying experience intense stress at the idea of flying. They are not only overwhelmed during the flight but also when choosing their flight, during the preparation of luggage or while making the trip to the airport. The fear of flying can be an isolated problem but sometimes finds its source in a problem of broader anxiety, such as claustrophobia, agoraphobia or dizziness.

Fear is considered a warning of potential danger: it puts us on alert to face the unknown. A considerable portion of people suffering from the fear of flying doesn't know how a plane works. When turbulence shakes it, they imagine that it can fall. Images of plane crashes feed their fearful emotions. Anxious people always imagine the worst, wherever they are, to calm their fears. It's the unexpected that scares them.

You certainly know that the deadliest means of transportation remain the car in front of the motorcycle, bicycle, bus, and train. The plane comes last in this ranking. Yet, it is the plane that has the focus of all of the flying phobia's anxieties.

In the following, we will go through some effective tips to overcoming a fear of flying.

Fatigue is an additional stressor. Try not to overload the program the day before your departure. Overcoming your fear can also require a lighter diet by avoiding all stimulants such as coffee, tea, sodas, alcohol, and even tranquilizers.

Take-off is often the most dreaded moment. So try to relax. Before boarding the plane, breathe slowly through the abdomen, listen to music or relax with a game on the phone. The takeoff lasts only three minutes; it's just a bad time that will pass; just avoid thinking about it.

Find a distraction.

Upon boarding, tell the staff on board about your fear of flying. They are trained to deal with this kind of situation, and there is no shame in that. To facilitate your discussions, book an aisle seat.

The fear of flying is primarily a fear of the unknown. And as for the famous air holes, they are like sea waves. They are not very comfortable, but they are perfectly safe. When you are in the water, you don't drown, you float. On the plane, it's the same thing. You cannot fall at once because there's the air. With its wings, the plane can even soar if a reactor stops. We saw it in 2009 when the pilot opted for an emergency landing on the Hudson River in New York.

An Airline Pilot is one of the most controlled professions. Although some feel it is not necessary, airline pilots are monitored twice a year. They are professionals. Every year, they undergo two inspections, one in a simulator and another in real conditions. Airline pilots are required to do a thorough medical examination each year.

Aviation is a routine form of travel. Each year two billion people partake in this form of transportation. Flying has become safer and more comfortable. It is a daily routine for some, recreational for others, and for some still, just an abstract concept they've only experienced through movies and television (usually dramatized), or something they've seen online.

Expose yourself gradually: start by looking at beautiful pictures of planes. For a while, avoid any pictures of plane accidents. Familiarize yourself with airports; go there for coffee for example. Then choose short flights and traveling with family or friends.

Above all, do not cancel your flight. This avoidant response is a known mechanism in psychology. However, the more you avoid something, the more your anxiety over it grows. Relax and take your boarding pass.

Ray Wood enjoys freelance, nonfiction essay work, blogging and other writing projects that feed his aspirations to leave the world better than he found it. Find him at www.raywood.info

The desire to fly... is handed down to us by our ancestors who, in their grueling travels across trackless lands in prehistoric times looked enviously on the birds soaring freely through space, at full speed, above all obstacles, on the infinite highway of the air.

Orville Wright

Fears and Phobias Galore

By Samantha Raes

Top 10 fears in the U.S. (8)

In a 2005 Gallup poll (U.S.A.), a national sample of adolescents between the ages of 13 and 17 was asked what they feared the most. The question was open-ended, and participants were able to say whatever they wanted. The top ten fears were, in order:

Terrorist attacks, spiders, death, being a failure, war, criminal or gang violence, being alone, the future, and nuclear war.

Top searched fears 2008

Book author Bill Tancer analyzed the most frequent online queries that involved the phrase, "fear of..." premised on the idea that people tend to search issues that concern them the most. His top ten list of fears queried in 2008 consisted of:

> flying, heights, clowns, intimacy, death, rejection, people, snakes, failure, and driving.

Common phobias

Several surveys indicate some of the most common fears are:

> Demons, ghosts, the existence of evil powers, cockroaches, spiders, snakes, heights, water, enclosed spaces, tunnels, bridges, needles, social rejection, failure, examinations.

The indisputable, number one fear across the board is:

public speaking. (8).

---

70 Most Common Phobias

These are some of the most common 70 phobias (though some are more common than others).

1) Arachnophobia—The fear of spiders.
2) Ophidiophobia—The fear of snakes.
3) Acrophobia—The fear of heights. Five percent of people suffer from this phobia.
4) Agoraphobia—The fear of open or crowded spaces. Sufferers can become homebound.
5) Cynophobia—The fear of dogs, including small and large breeds.
6) Astraphobia—The fear of thunder/lightning; AKA Brontophobia, and Tonitrophobia.
7) Claustrophobia—The fear of small and/or enclosed spaces, such as elevators.
8) Mysophobia—The fear of germs. AKA Germophobia or Bacteriophobia.
9) Aerophobia—The fear of flying. One of the most common fears.
10) Trypophobia—The fear of holes: more common than expected.
11) Carcinophobia—The fear of cancer. People with this can develop eccentric "health," regimens, filled with extreme diets, supplements and exercise, and an excess of health checkups and screenings.
12) Thanatophobia—The fear of death. Discussing it, even the thought of funerals and cemeteries can trigger this hyper-fear response.

13) Glossophobia—The extreme (beyond the normal) stifling fear of public speaking. It negatively impacts education and career.
14) Monophobia—The fear of isolation, even when eating or sleeping.
15) Atychiphobia—The fear of failure.
16) Ornithophobia—The fear of birds. Can be a broad or specific fear.
17) Alektorophobia—The fear of chickens.
18) Enochlophobia—The fear of crowds is related to Ochlophobia and Demophobia.
19) Aphenphosmphobia—The fear of intimacy. Can be expressed as a fear of tactile sensations (touch).
20) Trypanophobia—The fear of needles.
21) Anthropophobia—The fear of all kinds of people in all situations.
22) Aquaphobia—The fear of water, being in or around it.
23) Autophobia—The fear of abandonment and being abandoned.
24) Hemophobia—An extreme fear of blood.
25) Gamophobia—The fear of commitment or sticking with something to the end.
26) Hippopotomonstrosesquippedaliophobia–Fear of long words. Truth.
27) Xenophobia—The fear of the unknown, anything strange or foreign.
28) Basiphobia—The fear of falling. Some refuse to walk or stand.
29) Achievemephobia—The fear of success. Opposite of fear of failure.
30) Theophobia—The fear of God; causes an irrational fear of deity.
31) Ailurophobia—The fear of cats: also known as Gatophobia.
32) Metathesiophobia—The fear of change.

33) Globophobia—The fear of balloons.
34) Nyctophobia—The fear of darkness. A seemingly innate fear.
35) Androphobia—The fear of men.
36) Phobophobia—The fear of fear. The fear of being afraid of objects, people or situations.
37) Philophobia—The fear of love. Being scared of falling in or experiencing the emotions associated with love.
38) Triskaidekaphobia—The fear of the number 13, or at least the bad luck those afflicted believe is associated with it.
39) Emetophobia—Fear of vomiting and fear of loss of one's self-control.
40) Gephyrophobia—The fear of bridges.
41) Entomophobia—The fear of bugs and insects, also related to Acarophobia.
42) Lepidopterophobia—The fear of butterflies or other winged insects.
43) Panophobia—The fear of everything or fear of terrible things happening.
44) Podophobia—The fear of feet. Some fear touching or to look at them, even their own.
45) Paraskevidekatriaphobia—The fear of specifically, Friday the 13th.
46) Somniphobia—The fear of sleep. Being terrified of going to sleep.
47) Gynophobia —Fear of women. Related to unresolved mother issues.
48) Apiphobia—Fear of bees, specifically, the painful sting of this agitated or angry insect. Some may fear a severe allergic response.
49) Koumpounophobia—Fear of buttons. Clothes with them are avoided.
50) Anatidaephobia—The fear of ducks, specifically.

51) Pyrophobia—The fear of fire: a natural/primal fear that can be debilitating.
52) Ranidaphobia—The fear of frogs. Often caused by episodes from childhood.
53) Galeophobia—The fear of sharks in the ocean or even in swimming pools.
54) Athazagoraphobia—The fear of being forgotten or not remembering things.
55) Katsaridaphobia—The fear of cockroaches. Can lead to obsessive cleaning.
56) Iatrophobia—The fear of doctors. Do you delay doctor visits, or suddenly cancel appointments with no real explanation? You may have this.
57) Pediophobia—The fear of dolls.
58) Ichthyophobia—The fear of fish. Includes small, large, dead, and living fish.
59) Achondroplasiaphobia—The fear of midgets seems to stem from the "different," physical size/appearance.
60) Mottephobia—Fear of moths. They are only beautiful to some.
61) Zoophobia—The fear of animals. Applies to ALL animals.
62) Bananaphobia—The fear of bananas. (Truth.)
63) Scelerophobia—The fear of burglars, attackers or crime in general.
64) Cibophobia—The fear of food. May be related to fear of choking.
65) Phasmophobia—The fear of ghosts. AKA Spectrophobia.
66) Equinophobia—The fear of horses. Animal phobias are common.
67) Musophobia—The fear of mice. Some people find mice cute, but phobics do not in the least.
68) Catoptrophobia—The fear of mirrors. Being afraid of your reflection.

69) Telephonophobia—The fear of talking on the phone. Phobics prefer texting.
70) Pogonophobia—The fear of beards or bearded men.

Samantha Raes is a rosarian by heart and a would-be writer by vocation. She collects vintage jewelry, especially cameos, and loves anything and everything turquoise.

I am afraid of others knowing what I am afraid of.
Unknown

Poetic Pause

Poetry Pebbles

I decided that it was not wisdom that enabled poets to write their poetry, but a kind of instinct or inspiration, such as you find in seers and prophets who deliver all their sublime messages without knowing in the least what they mean.

Socrates

In a meadow full of flowers, you cannot walk through and breathe those smells and see all those colors and remain angry.
We have to support the beauty, the poetry, of life.

Jonas Mekas

Fear, a Monster

By Cesar Moran-Cahusac

Fear is the master, and it's the harshest one
The unique silent energy drainer that seizes us by the guts
A loathsome creature with a thousand faces,
That creeps upon us like a horror fairy tale anaconda,
Mimicking itself in any terrain; slick, slimy and powerful,
It's the lethal beast we have to conquer!
It follows us stealthy, along fields and dark orchards
When we move towards the arch of the door, it growls fiercely
Then in lightning spring snatches us by the face
Drowning our voice, that turns into a muffled yelp
Then it coils its tubular self around us, tight and abrasive
Doing so just to brand in us deeply all its façades.
By hypnotizing with a hiss a curse that makes us dormant,
Transforming us into static statues that suffer and sweat pearls
Painful ones that drip forcefully through our pores
That is when we believe we have to:
Fear to grow, to become and share
Fear to love, to expose and care,
Fear to do, to move ahead, to fail and learn
Fear to commit, to engage, to relate,
Fear to fall to pieces, to knead experiences to construct
Fear to be present and blossom spontaneously like spring fever
Fear to be unique like the constellations in the heavens
Fear to say hello, to smile and share peace
Fear to hug, to embrace ocean waves as sea foam stings our eyes
Fear to dance in freedom, so arousal instigates desires

Being in fear to be festive, so joy takes us to the skies
Fear is the paralyzer, and fear is what makes us alive
Once we unveil it; exposing dear vulnerabilities, our secret charms
Is when the master surrenders, the shadows dissipate,
The stuck in mud becomes a playful endeavor
We become theatrically invincible; the audience yields in awe
As we walk the dreamy meadow where lighting strikes
The dicey path to take to become a radiant superstar.

Cesar Moran-Cahusac is an ecologist, peace advocate and martial artist whose poetry weaves an expansive range of exotic, sensual and surprising life experiences into a dance of verbal refinement. He is the author of the popular poetry book entitled "She Said No to the Wind."

The most important vision one can have is a vivid and stunning glimpse of our own eternal, bright potential. Awareness of this Light within us, as well as others, ultimately leads to a positive, life-changing paradigm shift that is an essential milestone on our very long, very old, glorious journey.
It is a shift of faith and hope and love. A shift of courage.
A shift of focus, strength, and stamina.
A shift of everything we believe.
It is a shift of everything we are, we do, and hope to become.
This visionary reveal of our true self-inspires a complete change of everything we worry for, work for and want for.

Connie Kerbs

CHAPTER 5

A Literary Legacy

Inspired

Reflect upon your present blessings, of which every man has plenty; Not on your past misfortunes, of which all men have some.

Charles Dickens

But, all this while, I was giving myself very unnecessary alarm. Providence had mediated better things for me than I could possibly imagine for myself.

Nathaniel Hawthorne, The Scarlet Letter

To live in the world of creation—to get into it and stay in it—to frequent it and haunt it—to think intensely and fruitfully—to woo combinations and inspirations into being by a depth and continuity of attention and meditation—this is the only thing.

Henry James, Notebook

She will not sleep, for fear of dreams,
But, rising, quits her restless bed,
And walks where some be clouded beams
Of moonlight through the hall are shed.

Charlotte Brontë

A man that flies from his fear may find that he has only taken a short cut to meet it.

J.R.R. Tolkien, The Children of Húrin

The Boneyard Boys

By Connie Kerbs

A Literary Jaunt on THE Universal Fear: DEATH

At the close of his famous poem, Gray described, simply and movingly, what sort of man he believed himself to be, how he had fared in his passage through the world, and what he hoped for from eternity.

R. W. Ketton-Cremer (1955)

In the early 18th Century a peculiar literary niche was born which spurred a mournful fixation on the FEARS and sorrows all of humanity understands about death. These tender expressions of universal bereavement were defining and profound. The emotions they spoke to are still looked upon with respect and appreciation two-plus centuries later.

The impact this group of poets had on the literary landscape is immeasurable. Their melancholy questions provoked poignant emotions which paved even wider cultural paths of creative expression. They even played their part helping usher in the subsequent era known as the Romantic Period.

Sometimes referred to as The Graveyard School, the cluster of poetry and its authors consisted largely of emulations of the first few pieces. *A Night-Piece on Death*, widely credited as the first "Graveyard Poem," was published in 1721/22. The poem was described as an extension of its author, Thomas Parnell, described as a charming personality, with an uncanny ability to add a touch of class to lowly places and basal ideas.

There are two others topping the short list of earliest influences: Robert Blair's long poem, *The Grave* (1743), a charming 3mix of the macabre, and Edward Young's, dramatic blank-verse,

Night Thoughts (1742–45). These are literary paths of profound grief, which speak to the universal pain of mourning while reminding us of the conflicting repugnancy we naturally feel about the undeniably grotesque, physical process of death.

The philosophical meditations of the graveyard poets were never more sublimely expressed than in Thomas Gray's "An Elegy Written in a Country Church Yard" (1751). The poem is a dignified, generous eulogy celebrating the graves of humble villagers. It more than hints at the idea (considered novel and eccentric for the time) that the lives of rich and poor alike "lead but to the grave." In other words, death is the great equalizer of us all. It is the ONE and only, most ubiquitous FEAR.

The Great Equalizer

While these concerns wax and wane—culturally and individually—they never truly dissipate. We are ever reminded of them through the passages of life we all eventually experience, at least if we live very long. The loss of friends and loved ones to this mysterious, supposed enemy is the ultimate evidence of our own mortality. Of course, there are many other hints of these all around us. Such descriptions of death beheld in some of these lines are, as glorious as they are stark, emotional reminders we can't seem to avoid simply all of our *finite* lives.

These fears ever surround our inescapable passage beyond this existence—and goad the questions and anxieties we all have about life's true purposes. The biggest questions of all humanity: *What is it all for? What's next?* And, *What are the conditions (if any) on the other side?* Despite the greatest hope and belief any of us may aspire to have—that is all we actually can do: *hope*, the very definition of faith. All this as opposed to *knowing*.

So few of us have a concrete *knowing* (lest it would by definition, not be *faith*, but knowledge) of what details await us on the other side of this gate of no return. Those no few in number who have claimed sure knowledge on such matters have been either declared prophets, heretics, insane, charlatans or at the very least, imaginative dreamers. Personal ideology, religious background, and spiritual sensitivities we have each been uniquely equipped with, all help us filter the merit of such claims. This known reality is the core subject matter for the Graveyard Poets.

This unique cluster of literary path pavers was also known as the "Churchyard Poets," or more humorously—the "Boneyard Boys." Only time would afford this talented group of pre-Romantic English poets the recognition they arguably deserved. Their penned passages were commonly lambasted as overly gloomy, especially in their own era, and for a full century following their work. Thankfully, it persevered as any great work of any genre, style or type must do in the end.

The longer view of history has a distinct opportunity to tell a broader truth, from a collective response over time to any particular artist, creative process or approach to life. The decades rolling into centuries offer a far more complex and varied assessment of any particular work, or genre for that matter.

The collection of which we write about here brims with powerful, accessible, deliberations by this group of poetic, would-be philosophers. Yes, per the usual, they were by and large taken for granted and far too easily dismissed in their own time. But, history would eventually prove more than generous to the notorious *Boneyard Boys*, even if in long-delayed fashion, as was so often customary in the world of such literary giants.

Yes, they were oft scoffed by some in their day, (and still ours), for being too trite, too demented or too sentimental. Yet, the list is long and growing, of wholehearted acknowledgments for the deep resonance they once stirred, quietly, in open-minded circles. As now, there were those back then who embraced new ideas and who could appreciate new takes on very old themes. The proof persists, as their work continues showing it has the universal chops and resonance to echo loudly onto the modern stage.

None of the long-dead-acclaimed-clan would ever know themselves by any of their modern nicknames, by the way. The term *Graveyard Poets* wasn't even heard of until 1898, first coined in an article by the esteemed William Macneile Dixon.

This literary movement emerged with the religious revival that marked the early eighteenth-century. It was a time of spiritual confusion, crisis, and rebirth; it's no surprise that ruminations on death, and life, ghosts, and graveyards, were thematic subjects especially drawn to, in all their somberness.

Many of the Graveyard Poets were Christian clergymen, and so wrote moral-driven verse. They combined symbolism, and landscape with religious and philosophical instruction. They were inclined toward filtering subjects through life-after-death lenses which reflected man's (eternal) relation to the divine.

The mid-eighteenth century religious culture also included an emphasis on private devotion, as well as denoting an end to the long-standing accepted form of scripted funeral sermons. Each of these conditions demanded a new kind of text with which people could ponder life and death in a personal setting. Graveyard Poetry met that need, and so the poems were embraced, especially by the increasingly educated middle class. The Privilege of Piety

It helps to understand this eclectic group. For the first time in all the history of the world as we know it, there was a slice of (western) civilization with the privilege of being collectively literate. And they hungered for a variety of meaningful forms of written expression. They thirsted for fresh, inspiring writings that stimulated their intellect, as well as their hearts and souls.

For instance, Elizabeth Rowe's *Friendship in Death: In Twenty Letters from the Dead to the Living*, published in 1728, had 27 editions by 1760. This popularity, as Parisot says, "confirms the fashionable mid-century taste for mournful piety."

The works of the Graveyard School were essentially an introduction to the Gothic novel, contributing to the dark, mysterious mood and storylines that characterize the genre. Graveyard Schoolers focused their writings on the lives of ordinary and mysterious characters. Widely considered pre-Romanticists who helped usher in the Romantic literary movement, they did so by their reflection on emotional states. This is most transparent in Coleridge's "Dejection: An Ode" and Keats' "Ode on Melancholy."

The Graveyard Poets were influential figures who piqued brain and public mind. They were just the path emotions swelling for ages needed to alter the cultural landscape forever. They were a tell-tale crowd that spurred and demarked a sincere shift in mood and form in English poetry. Their influence was widespread and continued throughout the latter 18th century.

Widely considered the primary poem that ushered in the influential Graveyard School, and its poetic pupils, Thomas Parnell's *A Night-Piece on Death* follows.

Here is a quality list of some of the more well-known Graveyard Poets:

Thomas Parnell,   *Robert Blair*
Thomas Warton   *William Collins*
Thomas Percy   *Thomas Chatterton*
Thomas Gray   *Mark Akenside*
Oliver Goldsmith,   *Joseph Warton*
William Cowper   *Henry Kirke White*
Christopher Smart   *Edward Young*
James MacPherson   *James*

Deaths but a path that must be trod, if man would ever pass to God.
Thomas Parnell

A Night-Piece on Death

By Thomas Parnell

Introduction and Background

This work by Thomas Parnell, published posthumously in 1721 or 1722, is the earliest example of its kind, thus inspiring what would later be known as the Graveyard School of Poets. (9). The poem, a rhyming couplet in iambic tetrameter offers a gentle rhythm to back its profound, and for the day, considerably novel premise: which was in summary, *death is nothing to fear.*

The piece affords a rich excursion through the pensive environment it is set in the hues of nighttime in an old quiet church graveyard among all the humble tombs and markers. Its ultimate subject: the higher meaning and purpose of death. The poem is also a comment on the perceived, but unrealistic importance of each individual life, as noted by the vain monuments, (sepulchers, tombstones, and behemoth markers), which littered the graveyard

All of this stirred a poignancy in Parnell on the implied silliness of such ambitions given the shortness of our lives, and what we actually ever truly accomplish here, rich, poor, old or young. The poem goes on to offer an engaged reader an important and unique, paradigm shift: to consider with honest piety, that death is but a release from the prison, darkness, and futility that we know as our living state or current existence.

All nihilistic or suicidal ideations aside, the poem is almost a celebration of this idea and speaks to the familiar, transitory state of life we will rejoice to be freed from. The poem indicates a moving onto much better things, all that has little to do with any of the anxieties and fears humanity's mystique surrounding death and dying has perpetrated upon us. Parnell speaks eloquently to the progressive (for his time) idea that death is the doorway, which we emerge through, overwhelmed from the brightness of heaven we will suddenly find ourselves in.

So, while the poetry hints at a dark and melancholy setting, tone and point, it speaks to so much more than the dreaded, dreary subject, only rarely written about before its time—and then usually only in macabre depressing undertones at best.

To hear the poem, please check out the following link:

https://www.dropbox.com/s/hzktnc77hy-ojwyz/RG%20Thomas%20Parnell%20Night%20Piece.mp3?dl=0

Influence

A Night Piece on Death ultimately influenced a generation of poets, who would become known, more than a century after-their-fact, as the Graveyard Poets, or the Graveyard School. Starting with this piece, and the group's collective contribution it helped inspire, the foundation was formed for several whole genres. Entire schools of thought would eventually build upon its provocative (for the day) thought process.

It could be said this piece literally paved the way for Bierce, Poe and a slew of other highly influential, darker writers; literary pillars even, finally leading up to contemporary household names. The modern *kings* of literature, theater, art, and music cannot deny they owe a considerable portion of their platforms to the enlightened, visionary through the heavy words which follow.

Before all of that, though, this foundational piece, and others by the Graveyard Poets, (or Boneyard Boys), played a key role in the driving cultural forces that ushered in a whole new era: just a *little thing*, that would eventually be known as the *Romantic Period*. It is an exquisite example of the emotions and power a few well-written words can exert over time.

While reading this, it is especially fascinating to appreciate the advanced articulation this piece spoke to at a time when so few, if any quite like this had really dared to do so. Parnell speaks to a nuance of the struggles and sentiments universally felt with death. These were pioneering subjects for poetry and literature when it was penned, so precociously, decades ahead of its time.

A Night Piece on Death

By the blue taper's trembling light,
No more I waste the wakeful night,
Intent with endless view to pore
The schoolmen and the sages o'er:
Their books from wisdom widely stray,
Or point at best the longest way.
I'll seek a readier path, and go
Where wisdom's surely taught below.
How deep yon azure dyes the sky,
Where orbs of gold unnumbered lie,
While through their ranks in silver pride
The nether crescent seems to glide.
The slumb'ring breeze forgets to breathe,
The lake is smooth and clear beneath,
Where once again the spangled show
Descends to meet our eyes below.
The grounds, which on the right aspire,
In dimness from the view retire:
The left presents a place of graves,
Whose wall the silent water laves.
That steeple guides thy doubtful sight
Among the livid gleams of night.
There pass, with melancholy state,
By all the solemn heaps of fate,

And think, as softly-sad you tread
Above the venerable dead,
"Time was, like thee, they life possessed,
And time shall be, that thou shalt rest."

The church at Stoke Poges; (Fellow Graveyard Poet) Thomas Gray's tomb is at the foot of the brick-built extension on the left.
https://en.wikipedia.org/wiki/Elegy_Written_in_a_Country_Churchyard.

Those graves, with bending Osier bound,
That nameless heave the crumpled ground,
Quick to the glancing thought disclose
Where Toil and Poverty repose.
The flat smooth stones that bear a name,
The chisel's slender help to fame
(Which ere our set of friends decay
Their frequent steps may wear away),
A middle race of mortals own,
Men, half ambitious, all unknown.
The marble tombs that rise on high,
Whose dead in vaulted arches lie,
Whose pillars swell with sculptured stones,
Arms, angels, epitaphs, and bones,

These (all the poor remains of state)
Adorn the rich, or praise the great;
Who, while on earth in fame they live,
Are senseless of the fame they give.
Ha! while I gaze, pale Cynthia fades,
The bursting earth unveils the shades!
All slow and wan, and wrapped with shrouds,
They rise in visionary crowds,
And all with sober accent cry,
"Think, mortal, what it is to die."
Now from yon black and fun'ral yew,
That bathes the charnel-house with dew,
Methinks I hear a voice begin
(Ye Ravens, cease your croaking din,
Ye tolling clocks, no time resound
O'er the long lake and midnight ground);
It sends a peal of hollow groans,
Thus speaking from among the bones.
"When men my scythe and darts supply,
How great a King of Fears am I!
They view me like the last of things:
They make, and then they dread, my stings.

Eighteenth Century Tombs beneath the Yew tree at Stoke Poges. (Photo: Tony Grist.) https://commons.wikimedia.org/wiki/File:The_churchyard,_Stoke_Poges_

Fools! if you less provoked your fears,
No more my spectre-form appears.
Deaths but a path that must be trod,
If man would ever pass to God;
A port of calms, a state of ease
From the rough rage of swelling seas.
"Why then thy flowing sable stoles,
Deep pendant cypress, mourning poles,
Loose scarfs to fall athwart thy weeds,
Long palls, drawn hearses, covered steeds,
And plumes of black, that, as they tread,
Nod o'er the scutcheons of the dead?
"Nor can the parted body know,
Nor wants the soul, these forms of woe.
As men who long in prison dwell,
With lamps that glimmer round the cell,
Whene'er their suffering years are run,
Spring forth to greet the glitt'ring sun:
Such joy, though far transcending sense,
Have pious souls at parting hence.
On earth, and in the body placed,
A few, and evil, years they waste;
But when their chains are cast aside,
See the glad scene unfolding wide,
Clap the glad wing, and tow'r away,
And mingle with the blaze of day."

I am not afraid; I was born to do this.
Jeanne d'Arc (Joan of Arc, 1412—1431)

Fate's Irony

From an Ancient Talmud Text
Unknown Author

Appointment in Samarra, published in 1934, is the first novel by John O'Hara. It concerns the self-destruction of Julian English, once a member of the social elite of Gibbsville (O'Hara's fictionalized version of Pottsville, Pennsylvania). In 1998, the Modern Library ranked Appointment in Samarra 22nd on its list of the 100 best English-language novels of the 20th century. (4).

While I am neither endorsing nor disparaging this well-known work, its point here being the history behind O'Hara's choice of title. "Appointment in Samarra," is a reference to W. Somerset Maugham's retelling of an ancient Mesopotamian tale, which appears as an epigraph for the novel, of which a far older version is recorded in the Babylonian Talmud, Sukkah 53a.

It is a parable of sorts that speaks to the inevitability of death, and, perhaps even more than that—the inescapability of whatever fate has in mind for us. Both paradoxes being at the root of very specific, popular phobias, as well as the probable, silent, driving force behind entire clusters of anxiety.

Here is the little, demented, gem of fear of antiquity:

A merchant in Baghdad sends his servant to the marketplace for provisions. Shortly, the servant comes home white and trembling and tells the merchant he was jostled by a woman there; a woman whom he recognized as Death, and the servant goes on to describe her threatening gesture to him.

Borrowing the merchant's horse, he flees at top speed to Samarra, a distance around 75 miles (125 km), where he believes Death will not find him.

The merchant then goes to the marketplace and finds Death, and asks why she made the threatening gesture. She replies, "That was not a threatening gesture, it was only a start of surprise. I was astonished to see him in Baghdad, for I had an appointment with him tonight in Samarra." (10).

Do not let your fears choose your destiny.
Unknown

Poetic Pause

Poetry Pebbles

No man was ever yet a great poet, without being at the same time a profound philosopher. For poetry is the blossom and the fragrance of all human knowledge,
human thoughts, human passions, emotions, language...
Samuel Taylor Coleridge

Writing free verse is like playing tennis with the net down.
Robert Frost

A Rebuttal to the Boneyard Boys

By Henry Lawson (1892)

The Poets of The Tomb

The world has had enough of bards who wish that they were dead,
Tis time, the people passed a law to knock 'em on the head,
For 'twould be lovely if their friends granted the rest they crave,
Those bards Of "tears" and "vanished hopes,"…poets of the grave.
They say that life's an awful thing and full of care and gloom,
They talk of peace and restfulness connected with the tomb.

They say that man is made of dirt, and die, of course, he must;
But, all the same, a man is made of pretty solid dust,
There is a thing that they forget, so let it here be writ,
That some are made of common mud, and some are made of grit;
Some try to help the world along while others fret and fume
And wish that they were slumbering in the silence of the tomb.

'Twixt mother's arms and coffin-gear a man has work to do!
And if he does his very best he mostly worries through,
And while there is a wrong to right, while the world goes round,
An honest man alive is worth a million underground,
And yet, as long as she-oaks sigh and wattle-blossoms bloom,
The world shall hear the drivel of the poets of the tomb.

And though the graveyard poets long to vanish from the scene,
I notice that they mostly wish their resting-place kept green.
Now, were I rotting underground, I do not think I'd care
If wombats rooted on the ground or if the cows camped there;

And should I have some feelings left when I have gone before,
I think a ton of solid stone would hurt my feelings more.

Such wormy songs of moldy joys can give me no delight;
I'll take my chances with the world, I'd rather live and fight.
Tho' "fortune" laughs along my track, or wears her blackest frown,
I'll try to do the world some good before I tumble down.
Let's fight for things that ought to be and try to make 'em boom;
We cannot help mankind when we are ashes in the tomb. (11).

Henry Archibald Hertzberg Lawson (17 June 1867 – 2 September 1922) was an Australian writer and bush poet. Along with his contemporary Banjo Paterson, Lawson is among the best-known Australian poets and fiction writers of the colonial period and is often called Australia's "greatest short story writer." He was the son of the poet, publisher and feminist Louisa Lawson.

Remember, death is just the middle of a very long life.
An ancient Celtic proverb

CHAPTER 6

From The Mouths Of Babes

Inspired

Soft is a child's heart; Take care not to harden it.
Unknown

Grown-ups never understand anything by themselves, and it is tiresome for children to be always and forever explaining things to them.
Antoine de Saint-Exupéry

The three adventurers were overcome by that delicious weariness which suddenly overtakes one at the end of an outdoor day.
Carol Ryrie Brink, Caddie Woodlawn

Life isn't about finding yourself. Life is about creating yourself.
George Bernard Shaw

*I'll always say my prayers...and if God doesn't answer them...
I shall know it's because He's planning something
Better for me.*
Johanna Spyri, Heidi

How very little can be done under the spirit of fear.
Florence Nightingale

The Transfusion

Unknown

This story is from the time when blood transfusion technology was still in its infancy. It has stayed with me since my grandmother told it to me when I was quite young. Perhaps it resonated with me because I also have a little brother whom I felt devoted to—and still do.

There was a little boy who needed a simple blood transfusion to save his life. His "older," five or six-year-old sister was the only one with the right blood type that could be found quickly enough to save the little boy. When the doctor explained to her what needed to be done, and asked her if she was willing—she thoughtfully asked, "…so will this save my little brother's life?"

The doctor answered her with great hope, and so the children were soon readied for the procedure. As they lay side by side on the beds, and the transfusion began, the older sibling, obviously beyond her years, peered watchfully over her little brother—with little regard for any discomfort she may have had. As the transfusion progressed, the little girl began to lose some color, and she felt disoriented. The nurse checked on her and, though concerned, she tried to comfort and reassure the brave little girl. It was then, as she paled and grew weaker, the girl thought of herself for the first time since the procedure began, and she asked the nurse, "Will it take long to die now?"

That moment, of course, is when it was realized the little girl had thought the plan all along—which she had wholeheartedly obliged with—had been the giving of all of her blood to her brother in the ultimate sacrifice. The poignancy of her courage, unquestioning selflessness, and unreserved dedication to her brother made an indelible mark upon my heart. As did her undaunted decision, right up to the very end, to allow love to eclipse all her fear.

NOTE: An internet search for the original source of this story hasn't been definitive, but has brought up several variations, from all over the world. Some versions have boys instead of girls; all with only hints and hearsays of potential original sources, much later than I originally heard it from my own grandmother in the early 1970's. My conclusion is that she told it, probably based off an old film she would have seen sometime earlier in her life—much earlier: The 1925 Mary Pickford film, Little Annie Rooney. Whether all that follows sprung forth from that creation or whether even it was inspired by an even earlier telli9ng – it is nevertheless an intriguing little narrative, as enduring and mysterious as its original origins

---

Doubt, fear, and helplessness will always try to flourish when we are in a holding pattern for too long. The best defense is just to
DO something.
Something positive! Something healthy! Get moving!
Get busy in something worthy and meaningful and progressive!
Even if you are not specifically where you need to be yet, a step in the right direction is so much better than feeling mired in an endless rut, standing still.
Often, this is the only way to calm the inner storm.
Often, this is the only way the best course of action can reveal itself!
Further, this is the only way we will recognize the answers and solutions that might have been staring us right in the face all along.

Connie Kerbs

Fear of…

By Emilia Tupy

Fear is everywhere.
What are you afraid of?
Do you have a fear of heights?
A fear of losing loved ones?
A fear of the dark?
A fear of being alone?

We all have a fear even if we hate to admit it.

I'm afraid of clowns.
Their laugh is frightening.
Their eyes are too big to be real.
The makeup with blood red lips scares me.
They are too happy.
They haunt my dreams.

So, what are you afraid of?

Emilia Tupy is 10 and loves singing, dancing, acting, and writing. She also loves playing Minecraft and can often be seen on YouTube demonstrating her skills on video games under the pseudonym "cute lol."

Poetic Pause

Poetry Pebbles

Poetry is the opening and closing of a door, leaving those who look through to guess about what is seen during the moment.

Carl Sandburg, Good Morning, America (1928)

A good poem helps to change the shape and significance of the universe, helps to extend everyone's knowledge of himself and the world around him.

Dylan Thomas

If-

By Rudyard Kipling

https://en.wikipedia.org/wiki/If%E2%80%94#/media/
File:Kipling_If_(Doubleday_1910).

If you can keep your head when all about you
Are losing theirs and blaming it on you;
If you can trust yourself when all men doubt you,
But make allowance for their doubting too;
If you can wait and not be tired by waiting,
Or being lied about, don't deal in lies,
Or being hated, don't give way to hating,

And yet don't look too good, nor talk too wise:
If you can dream, and not make dreams your master;
If you can think, and not make thoughts your aim;
If you can meet with Triumph and Disaster
And treat those two imposters just the same;
If you can bear to hear the truth you've spoken
Twisted by knaves to make a trap for fools,
Or watch the things you gave your life to, broken,
And stoop and build 'em up with worn-out tools;

If you can make one heap of all your winnings
And risk it on one turn of pitch-and-toss,
And lose, and start again at your beginnings
And never breathe a word about your loss;
If you can force your heart and nerve and sinew
To serve your turn long after they are gone,
And so hold on when there is nothing in you
Except the Will which says to them: "Hold on!"

If you can talk with crowds and keep your virtue,
Or walk with kings, nor lose the common touch,
If neither foes nor loving friends can hurt you,
If all men count with you, but none too much;
If you can fill the unforgiving minute
With sixty seconds' worth of distance run,
Yours is the Earth and everything that's in it,
And, which is more, you'll be a Man, my son!

"If—" is a poem by British Nobel laureate Rudyard Kipling, written in 1895, and first published in Rewards and Fairies, 1910. It is a tribute to Leander Starr Jameson. The poem is written in the form of paternal advice to the poet's son, John. As poetry, "If—" is a literary example of Victorian-era stoicism. (11).

Kipling said that his poetic inspiration for the poem was the military actions of Leander Starr Jameson, leader of the failed Jameson Raid (December 1895 – January 1896) against the Transvaal Republic to overthrow the Boer Government of Paul Kruger some 15 years prior to its publication. The failure of that mercenary coup d'état aggravated the political tensions between Great Britain and the Boers, which led to the Second Boer War (1899–1902).

The cover of the first edition of The Jungle Book (1894).

https://en.wikipedia.org/wiki/Rudyard_Kipling#/media/File:Jungle_book_1894_138.jpg

As an evocation of Victorian-era stoicism—the "stiff upper lip" self-discipline, which popular culture rendered into a British national virtue and character trait, "If—" remains a cultural touchstone. The British cultural-artifact status of the poem is evidenced by the parodies of the poem, and by its popularity among Britons.

In India, a framed copy of the poem was affixed to the wall before the study desk in the cabins of the officer cadets at the National Defence Academy, at Pune and Indian Naval Academy, at Ezhimala.

In Britain, the third and fourth lines of the second stanza of the poem: "If you can meet with Triumph and Disaster/And treat those two impostors just the same" are written on the wall of the players' entrance to the Centre Court at the All England Lawn Tennis and Croquet Club, where the Wimbledon Championships are held.

The poem is quoted in the 1979 film, Apocalypse Now by the photographer played by Dennis Hopper.

An abbreviation of the poem is quoted in White Squall (1996) by McCrea, the English teacher (John Savage).

Bridget Jones was powerfully struck by "If-": "Poem is good. Very good, almost like a self-help book."

In 2016, the Boston Red Sox used the poem for a video tribute to retiring player, David Ortiz, narrated by Kevin Spacey.

The first lines of the poem are quoted in the 2015 film Mission: Impossible – Rogue Nation, as a password.

Joseph Rudyard Kipling, (1865 – 1936), was an English journalist, poet, and novelist.

Kipling's works of fiction include The Jungle Book (1894), Kim (1901), and many short stories, including "The Man Who Would Be King" (1888). Among his other poems, one finds "Mandalay" (1890), "Gunga Din" (1890), "The Gods of the Copybook Headings" (1919), and "The White Man's Burden" (1899). He is regarded as a major innovator in the art of the short story; his children's books are considered the world over to be iconic classics.

Rudyard Kipling by George Wylie Hutchinson
https://en.wikipedia.org/wiki/Rudyard_Kipling

Henry James said of him "Kipling strikes me personally as the most complete man of genius, as distinct from fine intelligence, that I have ever known." In 1907, at the age of 42, he was awarded the Nobel Prize in Literature, making him the first English-language writer to receive the prize and its youngest recipient to date. He was also sounded out for the British Poet Laureateship and on several occasions for a knighthood, both of which he declined.

In the context of the 20th century's waning imperialism, Kipling is an interpreter of sorts - of how the *empire* was experienced. That and the widely appreciated gift for his narrative talents make him a rare and special literary force. (12).

Words are, of course, the most powerful drug used by mankind.

Rudyard Kipling

CHAPTER 7

Mustard Seeds

Inspired

"And Jesus said unto them...
If ye have faith as a grain of mustard-seed...
Nothing shall be impossible unto you."
Matthew 17:20 (KJV)

Now faith is the substance of things hoped for,
the evidence of things not seen.
Hebrews 11:1 (KJV)

I sought to hear the voice of God
And climbed the topmost steeple,
But God declared: "Go down again—
I dwell among the people."
John Henry Newman

And all things, whatsoever ye shall ask in prayer,
believing, ye shall receive.
Matthew 21:22

Trust in the LORD with all thine heart;
And lean not unto thine own understanding.
Proverbs 3:5-6

Supplications

By Connie Kerbs

Paths of Fear explores a wide variety of fears through a diverse community of voices. This project hones out a portal offering a deeper, longer look at this basic emotion and how it impacts our life experience. It offers a bird's eye view of how people differ in their response to fear, and some of the variety of its aftermath. An important idea also explored here is how our reaction to it impacts the outcomes of our experiences, for good and for otherwise. Here in Mustard Seeds, we explore a different, facet of fear: a consideration of faith-based perspectives in dealing with some of the very hard things in life.

I submit to you now that our God, our Heavenly Father, longs eternal for our success and happiness, more than we can even begin to imagine at this point on our existent journey. He is ever moving us toward marvelous works that burn with anticipation at our core; wonders beyond our wildest dreams, and miraculous things we were created for in the first place.

I believe we get a minuscule taste of this Omnipotent desire in many ways. A concentrated one is through parenting, as we pine to see our own children grow and succeed. We yearn in our very bones for them to overcome all those things which we either must not or cannot protect them from. I am suspect one must look far and wide to find a better arena in which we can get a closer glimpse of how our Creator might feel towards us than through the children in our own life.

Capable parents, (teachers, and mentors), everywhere also do everything in their power to set their charges up for success and opportunity—as does our loving God. The best parents also offer to their children, all their lives, as much love, and support as they can muster—which is often an extraordinary sum-total, respectively. As does our Divine Creator, respectively.

Indeed, His contributions to our well-being, success and growth experiences are exponentially beyond our mortal comprehension.

Mustard Seeds are a beloved, metaphorical reference from the New Testament, (from Matthew 17:20 and Luke 17:6). As its namesake indicates, this chapter is a deliberation - an analogous testimony of sorts. I hope for it to be accessible and useful by a wide swath of views, but I accept that it may be appreciated most by those who have a sincere, personal conviction in one form or another, of the world religion known as Christianity.

That being said, this author has spent many an hour in an effort of astute reflection, to accomplish a cohesive, widely palatable contribution to the larger projects—both the title in its entirety and the Pebbled Lane Series it is part of. It's been an endeavor of the heart to put together, that which might be inspiring not only to multiple bandwidths of the Christian experience—but beyond, to my brothers and sisters of the human fold. Truly, my heart envisions something accessible across the palette of experience that positive, compelling spirituality is.

In some deep place of hope, (I suppose as every author does), I contemplate the tender possibility of some small thing here positively affecting someone who never considered these things before. I have also imagined with determination in my heart, as I have poured over this project, that something here will reach some dear reader, and improve their state of being, if only in some small way. I have a powerful hope that these ideas will be spiritually uplifting to readers, and that they might offer some inspirational gem to be tucked away until needed.

Perhaps someone will peruse these pages who just needs a gentle reminder of these powerful little *mustard seeds* already planted within them; tiny little specks of faith, which are still there. Even if seemingly minuscule, dormant even, they are just waiting to be nurtured, fertilized, watered and given some Light.

As well, the passions about these things stir in me to connect with others on these ideas. Not just anyone. This work seeks hearts and souls from all walks of life: those who need no convincing and who can (and likely do) spiritually inspire others around them all the time, as well as those who aren't convinced to any detail yet of what they believe about anything.

Then there are those who staunchly refuse any specific spiritual prescriptions, confident of their path. And others, in a similar reluctant religious camp, who would admit to the positive resonance they have felt a time or two before, unsure of its source or meaning—but somewhat accepting of its reality and existence. Albeit, they are curious, even if secretly, to understand it more.

Still, others have never felt it. While they are tenuous believers and even hope they will someday have the confirmation they desire, some of these *never-evers*, are reluctant to go all in with this idea. To their disappointment, their own spiritual experiences have never confirmed for them the anticipated, rewarding aspects of spirituality to which they feel they've been first promised, then denied.

These good people, while not comfortable wearing a decidedly atheistic badge of pride, have contemplated or even seriously flirted with the niche of agnosticism. They simply don't know how to feel about never having had a true "God," experience.

This interior experience is very common. It exists no matter what people might outwardly practice via cultural inheritance. It occurs alongside satisfactory participation in whatever subgroup, sector or niche of worship we spring from.

"If ye have faith as a grain of mustard seed... nothing shall be impossible unto you."

Others feel completely comfortable assigning the title of tender mercies to a daily walk with the help of divine intervention—or at least a kind of sincere, Omniscient interest. They have likely had an inexplicable yet satisfying, and diverse array of spiritual exposures. For them, it's easier, almost compelling to believe that spirituality is an essential aspect of the human experience, innate within all of us.

As for me, I believe it to be a part of us—a need that must be fulfilled as much as thirst, hunger, shelter, and a sense of belonging. Perhaps even more, lest all the rest be all for naught; lest there be no purpose or point, in the end, to any of anything.

Our spiritual needs are interconnected with all of these basic psychological and physical needs. These are inherent to the tribal wiring idea which whole passages here in *Paths of Fear* have spoken to, in one way or another, through several different voices.

For some, the spirit within feels like a healthy little green plant, bearing the fruit of its possessor's labors, rewarding all the attention it has been given. For others, it is a withering little stem that needs nurturing and nourishment to thrive again.

For still others, it is like a dormant seed that just needs the proper conditions to sprout.

I assert it is because we are, indeed, *ALL* His own. Whether we believe it or not. Whether we know it or not. Whether we admit it, or remember it or celebrate it, or not. Whether we *live* this, or not—we are part and parcel of the living proof of an intelligent, organized, purposeful creation. One of beauty and wisdom and intent beyond this ultimately limited view we see through the here and now.

These are precious matters to me, which emanate from my core, and while I am the last person to have all the answers or perhaps even very many at all, I am a soul who continually seeks them.

It is through this process I experience a continual kind of "smoothing," from the inside. I feel a sense of continual refining of my countless rough and unruly edges. This offers me a deeply satisfying layer of humility that softens any harshness and ignorant arrogance that sneaks up on me—which it does far more often than I realize, and far more often than I wish it did.

Indeed, it has been a long endeavor, an answered call from my heart to fulfill this project's purpose and scope. I can only hope now this simple testimony is all that it was supposed to be. I can only hope now its purpose will be fulfilled through the same Divine Design from which it was born in my soul. I can only hope now, this work will touch souls and lives, and be an instrument of help, hope, and healing.

I can only hope now it will be guided by His Hands—should He so choose to employ it in any way or for any purpose. I can only hope and pray that, as it is submitted to hearts willing to ponder upon these things, that they will in some way be succored and nurtured by them.

Fear thou not; for I am with thee: be not dismayed; for I am thy God: I will strengthen thee; yea, I will help thee; yea, I will uphold thee with the right hand of my righteousness.

Isaiah 41:10

Godly Fear

By Connie Kerbs

Not all Fears are Alike

It would seem to me as it has others, there is only one appropriate posture humankind has to our caring Divine Creator, our loving Father—our God. He is a most interested and patient Deity: an Omniscient Power. It goes without saying, our approach towards such a being would be one borne of the utmost, respect, and appreciation. Reverent, even. Words like overwhelming gratitude, and the kind of piety that makes one prostrate, as Peter felt on more than one occasion, resonate for many of us.

But there is more. Much more.

The Bible mentions *fearing* God throughout itself. A delightful verse that softens what I believe is this idea's most authentic tenderness on this subject is from Psalm 34. King David tells us about fearing the Lord as only King David can do:

> *"Come, you children, listen to me; I will teach you the fear of the LORD. ... Keep your tongue from evil, and your lips from speaking deceit. Depart from evil and do good; seek peace and pursue it."*
> *(Psalms: 34: 11, 13-14).*

And, King David, himself - again:

> *The fear of the LORD is the beginning of wisdom; a good understanding have all they who do His commandments. His praise endures forever.*
> *Psalm 111:10*

King Solomon explained it purely and simply like this:

The fear of the LORD is the beginning of knowledge.
Proverbs 1:7

There are numerous other references to our having a "fearful," relationship with God. These can be confusing to young, new, or barely believers. They are off-putting to the curiously- passing and are often a nudge in the negative direction to the reluctant or hesitant believer. Negative connotations which feed into the stereotypes of an angry god akin to (or worse!) than the mythical ones striding Mt. Olympus fuel the flames of the anti-religious. Atheist premises believe this validates their posturing against any omniscient presence – especially an angry, impatient or intolerant one.

However – this is important enough that we need to dig a little deeper here. First of all, there are many translation issues with a word like fear. Just like in our language there are many subtle shades of this emotional idea that, while similar, perhaps even from the same emotive resonance, they have important, unique nuances and connotations. For example, the words afraid, fear, panic, worried, fright, terrified, horror, thrill, concerned, tense, nervous, apprehensive, vexed, upset, incited, provoked, cross, frustrated, and anxious are all similar, and speak to the same emotional range. But, they have distinctively different meanings and usage. These aren't necessarily interchangeable, and their inflection is further crystallized when put into different contexts.

The Hebrew and Greek words used in the Bible for fear, have many different hues to them as well. In the context of fearing the Lord—their original intended meaning was almost always to convey a positive, and most appropriate *posture* towards a beloved God; namely an attitude of veneration, and respect believed to be owing, fair and square, to such a Creator.

The Hebrew verb *yare* (translated to *fear* from some of the original texts) was originally connected with the idea of "respect, & reverence." The Hebrew noun *yirah*, (another translated *fear* derivative), usually refers to a *"positively motivating* fear of God."

This kind of constructive fear credits the good of God's intent. It is inherent to God's commandments and helps a person be amenable to the wisdom to be had about Him, from Him, and through Him. While fear is the word used, it requires a broader understanding than the typical contemporary usage of that word.

The Greek noun, *phobos*, means "reverential fear" of God. This is not an ominous fear of His All-knowing, menacing power, or worry of some frightful, retaliatory punishment. Rather it is a *healthy dread* or fear of displeasing Him, not unlike that which a normal child might feel towards a parent they love, trust and do not want to disappoint fundamentally. It is more a sincere, pious desire to live up to certain positive expectations; a posture borne of love and gratitude for all that has been given more than anything else. This is the type of positive fear mentioned again and again throughout the New Testament by the Disciples like Luke, and especially by Paul.

A Love of the Law

John explains well that:

"God's love is expressed through his laws."

And, another nuance on our relationship to God, and how the giving and keeping of commandments binds us to him:

"For this is the love of God, that we keep His commandments. And His commandments are not burdensome."

1 John 5:3

So much of what Paul wrote spoke to this connection between God's love for us and the Commandments. It was also clarified in Paul's writings and the Gospels (See Romans 13:9-10; Matthew 22:37-40). It is here and many other references throughout the canon of scripture that this special, reverenced-based fear of the

Lord is designed to help us grow to become more like God—to grow in His love.

While respect and appreciation are the keys to any healthy, trust-based relationship, terror-style fear is not the posture our Creator wants us to have for Him. This fits with neither His prescriptions for us nor His judgment. I propose that anything akin to that negative kind of fear is a distortion of our loving Heavenly Father's original intent—which is far more gentle and natural in purpose and intent than we can actually fathom. Indeed, our God is wise.

In fact, I have a core, intrinsic belief his desire for us is entirely the opposite of anything compulsory or compelling upon us. While He is certainly sad, disappointed, even misportrayed as wrathful about us at times, as described in the ancient descriptions to the best of antiquities limited understanding of such Omniscience – all of it still falls under the parental umbrella; you know that mantel of passionate obligations which consumes us with a powerful desire to see our children be and do and become their very best.

And with all my heart, I believe it was never meant to coerce us, either subtly or fiercely into being anything we didn't want to be. Perhaps we just haven't always – and still don't – know what we don't know. All of which, of course, He knows.

He not only wants us to love Him, and embrace His commandments knowing they lead to our greatest happiness—but to do so of our own free will, not of His force, suffocating upon and around us.

God encourages us to take Him and His helpful laws seriously. Being in harmony with the spiritual laws that foster cooperation with others, and govern the universe, after all—has remarkable benefits. I stand unabashedly upon the old, "we have nothing to lose and everything to gain," soapbox.

Here are more verses clarifying the idea of Godly Fear:

Do not let your heart envy sinners, but be zealous for fear of the LORD all the day; for surely there is a hereafter, and your hope will not be cut off.
Proverbs 23:17-18

The fear of the LORD leads to life...he who has it will abide in satisfaction; he will not be visited with evil.
Proverbs 19:23

God is love 1 John 4:8), and His laws can be categorized into only two kinds: love for Him and love for fellow man
Matthew 22:37-40

Let us fear God, and keep his commandments; for that is the whole duty of everyone.
Ecclesiastes 12:13

For I am the LORD your God who takes hold of your right hand and says to you, Do not fear; I will help you.
Isaiah 41:13

Finally, God works to the end to etch His loving ideas upon our hearts. He aims that we understand Him, not for his sake, but ours; his omniscient goal being that we are not motivated solely by fear, but by our wholehearted love for him.

Fear is not to be overcome, or dreaded, or avoided, or expelled from our life; neither is it to be our dwelling, obsession or constant companion. It should be respected, recognized, and humbly listened to for its singular solemn advice. Fear was designed to function as a familiar adviser; rather than our foe, it is more that slightly overly honest, cautious, conservative friend. When it is accepted and appreciated for what it is, fear is a sage, a warning system, and one of our oldest, most experienced guides. When it holds itself at bay as necessary, it is the security detail that waits at some serious attention in the back of the room, ever watchful, ever ready, benign, non-threatening—until circumstances require its sensitive, timely services.

Connie Kerbs

Fear Not

By Connie Kerbs

We all, at some point in our lives, experience a deep-seated sense of fear. Those experienced with expressions of faith, however, have options to approach and allay their fears with spiritual perspectives.

A Framework

All positive religions I know of are built on the essential idea that we are not alone, that there are creative powers and forces beyond our complete understanding. It is beyond our reach at this stage of our long journey. These institutions also explain to us in a variety of ways and in a variety of details, how we are ever being guided and loved by that Omniscient force.

All of these walks of faith are laced with expressions of our potential appeal to that *energy*. They offer numerous why's, ways, and hows of our using it for the good of our life in the here and now. These religious constructs tell us that this intelligent force not only exists for good, and not only can but wants to improve upon our imperfectness. We are told again and again, how this force for good wants to improve and develop our lives and our souls.

In a general sense, we are taught of its hope and purpose of enhancing our own personal well-being. We know of its enrichment of our experience in this state—as well as the ways and means to do more of the same, and so much more in the next plane of existence.

Typically, we are taught through these religious paradigms, that in fact, this Creative Power has a salient purpose of encouraging us on our fallible, sometimes discouraging path. One of its key values is its built-in propensity to uplift us when we've fallen, to strengthen and heal us when we are physically or emotionally broken, and to help us realize more fully our own potential.

Much of the supplication and meditation (prayer) encouraged in these schools of thought are also about how this Higher Power helps us to actualize our transcendent capacities for the good of ourselves, the world around us, and others.

As we study these principles more deeply, in almost every one of these religious frameworks—we would discover a secondary message of how and why this all-powerful Being might be interested in us pitiful creatures. These schools of religious thought each attempt to offer insight as to how this Creative Omniscience might work in and through us promoting its own positive agendas.

Of course, we will find as many different proposals of what these purposes and truths might be, as there are unique churches. This doesn't diminish the message – in fact, it takes this idea to an archetypal level of experience within the human condition. Almost all people of all times and places have questioned and debated and pondered these big ideas – and postulated answers they could live with. Or, as some would be bold enough to say – some have been deeply inspired, even guided, to share their experiential discoveries on such weighty matters.

We could also learn at least some ideas on the means and ways these experiences are incredibly satiating and restorative in our life. Finally, we can glean insight as to how all of this can give us a purpose, fulfillment, and inspiration for our life unlike anything else can do.

What does all of this have to do with *Paths of Fear*, you say? Well—eventually this all leads to the idea that adversity faced with faith becomes a powerful impetus for positive growth and change. Studying those of our faith from the past, gently reminds us that bad times have not only been before—but they have always come and gone. This helps us to grasp a broader view and be a little less anxious about the end results. It helps us not to get too hung up on the negative experiences themselves, as they weave through our lives.

Simply put, as we grow in faith, and it permeates our understanding, encompassing all aspects of our life, more and more, fear will recede, and fail to maintain a foothold in our lives. It will take more and more of a proper, balanced place in our life—that of the background, instead of the foreground.

The fact is, though, all of this is often easier said than done. We are only human, and sometimes the balance between faith and fear becomes a struggle in our lives, as it did for those who came before—even the ones we look to for exemplary guidance.

For example, as did the disciples, as described in Matthew 8:25. And, remember, these guys had the embodied Icon, the Savior—one of the most powerful and influential beings of all time, literally, right by their side!

Remember when they encountered a furious storm in the boat on the Sea of Galilee? Their thoughts turned to fear. Jesus, who was sleeping at the time, was stirred up abruptly by the frightened disciples.

"Lord, save! We're going to drown!"

He replied, "You of little faith, why are you so afraid?"

Then he got up, rebuked the winds and the waves, and it became immediately and completely calm.

There are many stories in the Bible about courageous men and women facing the peril of sudden, unexpected storms like these—and how faith helps them go about it, get through it, and get over it. In other words—get back out on that boat again.

There are many other stories about the people who put everything on the line for something they believed—even if initially reluctant or afraid. They ultimately, by accessing their High Power, stepped up to the plate, in all their own ill-equipped conditions and imperfect, fallible natures. By mustering real strength and courage, despite any personal insecurity and self-doubt, they forged through all the obstacles, internal and external—and pleaded or fought with all they had on behalf of others.

The agendas of these folks centrally focused on the marginalized, persecuted, and downtrodden. They helped those who couldn't improve their own conditions without the aid of others—and whose odds of overcoming were virtually nil without the miracle only a Higher Power could realize. And when these heroes begged their personal cause, it was with the greatest humility, usually born of fear and grief for their circumstances. They usually have a sincere hope of either a rescuing to safety or newfound peace for those they feel responsible to, in context of whatever difficult conditions they face at hand.

Each of their particular details, and the actualization of their valiant faith and selflessness, in the end, resulted in the miracles needed. Their exemplary portrayals of grace and acceptance of what may come in their difficult circumstances were almost always attended by the real risk of the ultimate sacrifice of all they were, or hope to become. So profound their courage and faith, they inspire us still, somehow immortalized thousands of years after the fact. Here are some more common and a few lesser known examples.

> *When I am afraid, I put my trust in you.*
> Psalm 56:3

Claudia:

Claudia, wife of Pilate, after having heard the news of Jesus' arrest, was troubled in her sleep. Her dreams lead to the view that Jesus should be released, and on that fateful day, a messenger rushes in with a bold warning for Pilate from his wife.

Because of Pilate's own crippling political fears, he ignored both his personal reticence and Claudia's pleas. He pressed forward with the infamous sentencing of Jesus that would result in the most well-known, and influential martyrdom in all of history.

Besides the big obvious main story here – there is an important, less known side-story. The one of Claudia. In spite of her fears, and tremendous pressures she faced, she followed strong inspirations she had to stand up for someone far below her perceived status in the civilized world. Jesus. King of the Jews. Additionally, in all her unlikelihood, she was the only person who dared to face the powers that be, and make supplication for his release. Indeed, she was the only one we know of who made any real case for The Son of Man.

I prayed to the Lord, and he answered me.
He freed me from all my fears.
Psalm 34:4

David:

David was no stranger to fear. In Psalm 56:3 he says, *"When I am afraid I put my trust in you,"* referring of course to his faith in God. So when Goliath demanded that someone fight him, his response was:

"The LORD, who delivered me from the paw of the lion and the paw of the bear, will deliver me from the hand of this Philistine."
Samuel 17:37.

Of course, this early part of the Psalmist's story ends with young David's triumph against the mighty Goliath. This was not only a hefty personal victory – but one with the pressures of national, cultural and military significance for his people. In this time and place, they faced a considerable enemy who would prefer to enslave them, but would just as happily destroy the children of Abraham, the Israelites. He faced the giant with a simple sling and stone to which David, even as a boy, was no stranger – and swiftly took out the terrible foe who mocked him mercilessly.

Even though I walk through the darkest valley,
I will fear no evil, for you are with me.
Psalm 23:4

Esther

Esther was a Jewish woman selected by King Ahasuerus to be his wife by competition, and in part because of her great beauty.

However, he did not realize she was a Jew. As word spread that Haman, the king's right-hand man was devising a plan to kill the Jews, Esther's uncle Mordecai begged her, at the risk of capital punishment, to solicit the king to spare their life. (Wives then could only approach the king when summoned.)

> *"I will go to the king, even though it is against the law.*
> *And if I perish, I perish."*
> Esther 4.

Esther succeeded in winning the king's favor, and Haman's genocidal scheme was prevented as a result of her courage and bravery to approach her husband-King, on her people's behalf.

> *They do not fear bad news;*
> *they confidently trust the Lord to care for them.*
> Psalm 112:7

Job:

Remember Job's devotion to God? Satan came to God and told him that Job was only following God for his selfish gain, so God, for everyone's benefit, eventually even Job's—allowed him a test.

In one day, all of Job's ten children died, and he lost his great fortune. The second day he broke out in boils. His friends then turned against him, accusing him of some kind of sin he must have done to bring this all on himself. He still fell to the ground in worship and thanked God.

Even though he was subject to the most extreme discouragement one person could possibly know in such a short amount of time, he never succumbed to fear despite the worst problems imaginable. Job's exemplary faith under fire placed his story and legacy in the halls of time to be referenced milieus later.

Side-note: God restored everything to him in the end, and much more, because of his enduring faithfulness.

> *I am leaving you…peace of mind and heart.*
> *And the peace I give is a gift the world cannot give.*
> *So don't be troubled or afraid.*
> John 14:27

Deborah:

Deborah was a prophetess, judge, and wife of Lapidot, who led an outnumbered and badly equipped troop to a great victory. She sent for Barak, an able military general and told him that it was God's will that he should lead the forces.

> *"The Lord, the God of Israel, commands you:*
> *'Go, take with you ten thousand men of Naphtali and Zebulun*
> *and lead them up to Mount Tabor.*
> Judges 4

Barak agreed to lead only if Deborah, herself a great warrior, widely respected, accompanied him in battle. She agreed, and despite tremendous odds against them, they won.

The Bible makes a small reference to her fear over and again. *"Fear not,"* it says. While we can't always choose *what* fear we must grapple with, or *when*, or by *which* means we face it, we must choose our posture, our stance, our method—the *how* of our reaction to fear in our life.

> *The Lord is my light and my salvation--whom shall I fear?*
> *The Lord is the stronghold of my life—of whom shall I be afraid?*
> Psalm 27

This passage speaks to a sincere testimony and trusting in God, *no matter what happens.* Turning to God in our challenges makes a monumentally positive difference as to how and *if* we have a secure sense of overcoming our challenges. He knows our sorrows and fears—and cares infinitely about them. He truly understands our tedious insecurities, and our flaws. He knows in His universal wisdom that our believing in ourselves is pivotal to our success. He knows that faith in our ability to access what only He can offer wields us the greatest power in any battle we ever face.

Good Parents Allow Experience and Growth

Moreover, He offers us a strength we didn't even know we could access before. He shows us a force within we likely would have never even glimpsed without our trials in life. Because of this, while I don't believe he specifically *causes* our setbacks and disappointments, (that is, after all, *someone else's department*), He *allows* us to face the conditions that naturally occur and evolve in such an imperfect world full of flawed people, negative forces, and complex situations.

As our caring Creator, He understands, with infinite wisdom, our marvelous capacity to endure and aspire to success. Even if we are slow to discover and develop our inner selves, we have all along possessed their oft unappreciated potential.

Sometimes it is only after we have become truly too bruised, too broken or too discouraged to go on our own, that we finally become our most malleable in the Potter's hands. These times lend to a humility that helps us accept a positive faith.

By allowing us to struggle and strive to overcome we have the chance to turn to Him of our own accord, instead of by compulsion. In this way, our God gently nurtures our growth, potential, and capacity for understanding ourselves, others—and *Him*.

It is *then* He buffers circumstances and bridges gaps we could never clear on our own. He helps us to help ourselves, *through* Him. He urges us to help each other. *He* helps us in His own wisely chosen ways, both subtle, and overt. His miracles, minuscule and monumental are assuredly all around us if we will only choose to see them.

When I am afraid, I put my trust in you.

Psalm 56:3

Bible Verses On Fear

By Connie Kerbs

Here are a few of the over 500 Bible verses referencing, "fear."

But now, this is what the Lord says…Fear not, for I have redeemed you;
I have summoned you by name; you are mine.
Isaiah 43:1

Be strong and of good courage, fear not, nor be afraid of them: for
the LORD thy God, He it is that doth go with thee;
He will not fail thee, nor forsake thee.'
Deuteronomy 31:6

For ye have not received the spirit of bondage again to fear; but…the Spirit of
adoption, whereby we cry, Abba, Father.
Romans 8:15

I will say of the LORD, He is my refuge and my fortress:
my God; in him will I trust.
Psalm 91:2

Have not I commanded thee? Be strong and of good courage; be not afraid,
neither be thou dismayed: for the LORD thy God is with thee
whithersoever thou goest.
Joshuah 1:9

And who is he that will harm you, if ye be followers of that which is good? But
and if ye suffer for righteousness' sake, happy are ye: and be not
afraid…neither be troubled;
1 Peter 3: 13-14

In my distress, I cried unto the Lord, and he heard me.
Psalms 120:1

*I sought the LORD, and he heard me and delivered me
from all my fears.*
Psalms 34:4

*...We were troubled on every side; without were fightings, within were fears.
Nevertheless, God, that comforteth those that are cast down, comforted us...by
the consolation wherewith he was comforted in you...*
2 Corinthians 7: 2-7

*There is no fear in love, but perfect love casteth out fear:
because fear hath torment.
He that feareth is not made perfect in love.*
1 John 4:18

*In the multitude of my thoughts within me
thy comforts delight my soul.*
Psalms 94:19

*Peace I leave with you, my peace I give unto you: not as the world giveth, give I
unto you. Let not your heart be troubled, neither let it be afraid.*
John 14:27

*Take therefore no thought for the morrow: for the morrow shall take thought
for the things of itself. Sufficient unto the day is the evil thereof.*
Matthew 6:34

*Humble yourselves therefore under the mighty hand of God,
that he may exalt you in due time:
Casting all your care upon him; for he careth for you.*
1 Peter 5: 6-7

Poetic Pause

Poetry Pebbles

*I think that I shall never see
A poem lovely as a tree.
Poems are made by fools like me,
But only God can make a tree.*

Joyce Kilmer

Poetry's a mere drug, Sir.

George Farquhar (1698)

Abide With Me

By Henry Francis Lyte

Abide with me; fast falls the eventide;
The darkness deepens; Lord, with me abide;
When other helpers fail, and comforts flee,
The help of the helpless, oh, abide with me.

Swift to its close ebbs out life's little day;
Earth's joys grow dim; its glories pass away;
Change and decay in all around I see—
O Thou who changest not, abide with me.

I need Thy presence every passing hour;
What but Thy grace can foil the tempter's power?
Who, like Thyself, my guide and stay can be?
Through cloud and sunshine, Lord, abide with me.

I fear no foe, with Thee at hand to bless;
Ills have no weight, and tears no bitterness;
Where is death's sting? Where, grave, thy victory?
I triumph still if Thou abide with me.

Hold Thou Thy cross before my closing eyes;
Shine through the gloom and point me to the skies;
Heav'n's morning breaks, and earth's vain shadows flee;
In life, in death, O Lord, abide with me.

"Abide with Me" was composed by Henry Francis Lyte, a Scott, while he was bedridden in the final stages of tuberculosis. It is often put to the tune of William Henry Monk's "Eventide." It's inspired by Luke's touching, visual account of the sacrament in the New Testament, which is in Luke 24: 28 – 31:

And they drew nigh unto the village, whither they went: And He made as though He would have gone further. But they constrained Him, saying, Abide with us: For it is toward evening, and the day is far spent. And He went in to tarry with them. And it came to pass, as He sat at meat with them, He took bread and blessed [it], and brake, and gave to them. And their eyes were opened, and they knew Him; and he vanished out of their sight.

Luke 24: 28-31

When I hear music, I fear no danger. I am invulnerable. I see no foe. I am related to the earliest times, and to the latest.

Henry David Thoreau

Chapter 8

The Best Medicine

Inspired

We all have moments in our life where we must face overwhelming fear; when taking young, busy children to visit somewhere with impeccable housekeeping and light-colored décor or an elderly relative with a lifetime of precious knick-knacks strategically strewn about. Then there is the ultimate anxiety of all parents: when
their adolescents begin dating.

Connie Kerbs

The great question that has never been answered, and which I have not yet been able to answer, despite my thirty years of research into the feminine soul, is,
'What does a woman want?'

Sigmund Freud

I became insane, with long intervals of horrible sanity.

Edgar Allan Poe

An optimist may see the light where there is none,
but why must the pessimist always run to blow it out?

Rene Descartes

There is no such thing as paranoia.
Your worst fears can come true at any moment.

Hunter S. Thompson

Mortality Rates

By Nancy Raymond

Roger was afraid of (almost) everything. When his mother tried to wake him up in the morning, he shrunk back under his covers, reciting the statistic that over 450 people die falling out of bed annually. She rolled her eyes and grabbed his arm, dragging him up and pulling him to the center of the room. She tugged off his pajamas and then handed him clothes to get dressed, but he stood there in his underwear, arms crossed, and lips pouting.

"What if I get a rash?" he asked.

His mother's arm remained extended, clothes in hand until he finally took them and proceeded to get dressed. He didn't want to enter the bathroom to wash his face and brush his teeth. He was afraid that a nest of spiders was going to crawl out of the sink drain. He also knew it was only a matter of time before an alligator was going to find its way up through the plumbing and out of his toilet. With his luck, both would happen at the same time. His mother assured him that the likelihood, even the possibility, of these events was remote, but he begged her to stand beside him while he was in there. He kept a close eye on the sink, while she watched the toilet, just in case.

He went to school without breakfast that morning, because the daily battle took just a little too long to work through. He was just sure his morning meal was poisoned.

"Why would I poison your cereal?" his mother asked.

"Not *you*. But what if someone from the factory did it? How would you feel if you forced me to eat poisoned cereal?"

179

His mother sighed, rubbing the sides of her forehead. "Okay," she said, dumping his breakfast down the garbage disposal.

Before he put on his shoes, Roger turned them over and shook them to make sure that no deadly scorpions had crawled into them and were waiting there for his unsuspecting feet. He asked his mother to weigh his backpack before slipping it over his shoulders, as he didn't want to suffer from back pain later because it was too heavy.

Although Roger voiced his concerns each weekday morning at the death rate in America from motor vehicle accidents, he reluctantly got onto the long yellow bus that would transport him to his fifth-grade class at the elementary school. He was no longer allowed to sit in the first three rows, a specific request from the driver, Carol. Apparently, while she was pregnant, he decided to educate her on the infant mortality rate in this country, unusually high for such a developed nation and asked her if she had considered a home birth.

When the doors of the bus opened to the sidewalk in front of the school, Roger paused before disembarking.

"What's the matter, Roger?" a teacher on the sidewalk asked.

He stared at the ground, brow furrowed. "Just checking for cracks in the concrete," he said, and then looked up at her. "I don't want to trip and fall. I could break my neck, you know."

"Yes, Roger. I know."

At lunchtime, he took his place in line. The first lunch lady he reached asked him if he would like some meatloaf.

"To what temperature was it cooked?"

"I'm sorry?" she asked.

He repeated himself, "To what temperature was it cooked?"

Familiar with this line of questioning, she replied in a flat tone, "All food in this kitchen is cooked according to official food safety guidelines."

Roger paused. "Are you sure?"

She nodded.

"Okay," he said, and she placed the meat on his plate.

He sat alone in the corner of the cafeteria, slathering hand sanitizer onto his hands and forearms before beginning to eat. After he was finished, he needed to use the bathroom but decided he would wait until he got home. He never used the one at school; he was too afraid of the bacteria he could contract by using the same toilet as hundreds of other children. After all, schools were breeding grounds for all kinds of illnesses.

As he walked to his next class after lunch, he spotted the principal in the hallway and approached him.

"Principal Gorder!" he exclaimed.

"Hello there, Roger." The principal spoke to him in the same sort of voice that the lunch lady had used. It was a familiar tone to Roger by now.

"I was wondering about my petition regarding seat belts in the school buses for this district? Have you made any headway with the school board?"

Principal Gorder sighed. "Remember, Roger, we talked about this. It's not up to us. It's a state law. It doesn't go by the district."

"Did you hear about the recent bus crash in Texas?"

The principal nodded. "I did. It was an unfortunate incident."

"Three students died. It was very tragic," said Roger worriedly.

"Hmm," Roger said. "Well, I also wanted to mention that there's a crack in the sidewalk outside. Did you know about that? It could be grounds for a lawsuit, you know."

Gorder nodded again. "What would I do without you, Roger?" He glanced down the hallway. "You'd better get going. Don't want to be late!"

"Right, sir," Roger said. "Thank you for your time."

But Principal Gorder had already begun hurrying away in the opposite direction.

When Roger got home a few hours later, he removed a sheet of paper from his backpack and attached it to a clipboard.

"What's that?" his mother asked as she walked in.

"It's a list of products that have been recalled," he said proudly.

"Oh."

"I thought you might want it for when you go grocery shopping. It's something good to have on hand."

"That's true," she said, sighing.

"I'll compare it to what we have in the house, Okay, Mom?"

"You're a good boy, Roger," she said, sitting down with a sigh.

He looked up at her from his list and smiled.

"I know," he beamed, pulling a pen from his backpack, while grasping the clipboard, and began opening the cupboards, examining their contents.

When Nancy Raymond is not writing, she is writing. She loves poetry, classic literature, and non-fiction travel memoirs. She also enjoys biographies and autobiographies—and has ghostwritten several for successful publications.

The only thing to fear is fear itself...and spiders.
Be very afraid of spiders.
One Wise Proverb

Poetic Pause

Poetry Pebbles

*I would define, in brief, the Poetry of words as
The Rhythmical Creation of Beauty.*

Edgar Allan Poe, The Poetic Principle (1850)

*He who draws noble delights from sentiments of poetry is a true poet,
though he has never written a line in all his life.*

George Sand, The Haunted Pool (1890)

Scaredy-Cat

By Connie Kerbs

There was once a lady, who was a bit of this and some of that.
She was many things – but most of all she was a scaredy- cat.

Over the years, through some fearsome trial and error,
She figured out what caused her unbearable terror.

She controlled it for a while, and off and on, felt pretty good.
She accepted what NOT to read or watch, and what she could.

Now, she wasn't too afraid of just any old random thing.
It wasn't silly superstitions that got her imagination going.

It was that time of early light, that eerie space between night & day.
Where imagined zombies and vampires lingered to stalk their prey.

That time of deadly desperation for nocturnal monsters and fiends.
When the night's creatures bring their trickiest, wickedest means.

Sometimes she was fine; but the other times she would just hide.
Then - family movie night. They convinced her it was fine: They lied.

Horrible zombies everywhere! No one safe - everyone was turned!
The only hope was that sunlight melted them with 3rd-degree burns!

Oh no. She didn't leave or look away. After all, it was a great flick.
But then, the worst zombie got too smart, too strong, TOO quick.

You know this story. No one escapes. Even the sweet dog got dead.
Now, that worst zombie with the weird jaw, and the ugly bald head-

He stalks her windows every night; and sometimes even in the day.
Long after, scaredy-cat had to have a plan; she just had to hide away.

Finally, she got it controlled, got a routine down; and that was that.
She let the dog out early, petted and fed that back-porch kitty-cat.

In time, she relaxed. Then once, even though she really knew better-
In those weird wee hours just before dawn, she got up to get water.

The kitchen was close, after all. – "C'mon!" she said. "Just Do It!"
Such a mistake: that scary movie scene when the victim will rue it!

She reached the fawcett, avoiding the porch window over the sink.
She nervously filled her glass. "Don't worry, see? Just calmly drink."

Then, for just an instant, in that tricky light just before morning;
Oh no! It was over! Her scaredy-cat-heart attacked without warning!

A reflection, a flash, a hideous bald deformity had caught her eye.
Triggering her ticker to squeeze up and seize up - causing her to die.

When her family found her, they were shocked - thrown for a loop.
And as they came and went, they passed and petted that porch cat,
And they were extra sure to dodge the big globs of wild turkey poop.

I have great faith in fools; self-confidence my friends call it.
Edgar Allan Poe

Chapter 9

In Summary

Inspired

Just a moment of genuine support given in one's time of discouragement will usually do more good than hours of praise or countless compliments offered in easy times.
Connie Kerbs

The most fearful unbelief is unbelief in yourself.
Thomas Carlyle (born 1700s)

Standing on the bare ground— my head bathed by the blithe air, and uplifted into infinite space—all mean egotism vanishes. I become a transparent eyeball; I am nothing; I see all; the currents of the Universal being circulated through me; I am part or particle of God.
Ralph Waldo Emerson

A strong argument for the religion of Christ is this—that offenses against Charity are about the only ones which men on their death-beds can be made—not to understand—but to feel—as crime.
Edgar Allan Poe

Whoever loves becomes humble. Those who love have, so to speak, pawned a part of their narcissism.
Sigmund Freud

Never give up...No one knows what's going to happen next.
L. Frank Baum

Conclusions

By Connie Kerbs

It is vital that we accept that fear is a normal, even healthy part of life, but it is just as important to come to terms with our more serious, pressing fears, and that we have a sense of resolution about them.

Just as important, it is key to our success to feel a sense of control over any deep-seated fears that overcome us. In the end, we must have relief from what can become a toxic experience with such strong emotions in our life. Long-term dealing with these powerful feelings, at a negative, or out of control level, leads to depression, and a long list of other problems, physical, mental, emotional, and social—many of the things elaborated throughout this book.

The age-old wisdom of replacing fear and darkness with love and light is not new. But it is ever relevant. This love and light are the basis of virtually every positive religion and form its fundamental message. It is the main premise of all the sects of Christianity and is an essential component to every other major belief system I am aware of. It is the antithesis of all things negative that weigh us down.

In the New Testament, St. Paul wrote to encourage, all of us, specifically through Timothy:

> *For God gave us a spirit, not of fear,*
> *but of power, and love, and self-control.*

2 Timothy 1:7

Confucius, Socrates, Buddha, Moses, Isaiah, Christ, John, Peter, Dyer, Buscaglia, Mother Theresa—and countless others, have been resounding through time for as far back as we can know with the same basic message. From all corners of the globe—China, Greece, Europe, India the Americas, and now throughout the entire, ever-shrinking modern world, some of the same ideas continue to resonate regardless of language, time, religion, or culture. Just this:

Life need not be overwhelmed, dominated, controlled, guided or permeated by fear.

Our experiences need not be defined by fear. We have a great Light and Power within and around us. It lights our immediate path, as we attempt to plod forward through whatever obstacles that would hinder and stumble us in darkness. This Light also beams a bright splay upon the upcoming path, beyond the here and now.

We can rely on this Light, to guide us, to lean upon for a reprieve, and to live life to the fullest. We can encourage others to do the same. This increases our personal joy and expands our experiences and connections to their greatest potential.

This Light can shelter us and guide us with wisdom beyond our own. We can draw strength from it in our hour of discouragement and fatigue. We can count on it to help us change direction—physically, mentally, emotionally and spiritually.

This Light encourages and energizes us with the strength to press on, as well as many other mighty and marvelous things it will do for us. It is only incumbent upon us to want it, to trust it, and to believe in it with only the smallest measure of faith.

This Power affords us discernment and peaceful acceptance of all circumstances that find us. It is the inspiration behind our healing need to forgive others—and ourselves.

It is also a path of miraculous change —big and small.

The reliable guidance to be found is indescribable, if we embrace it, trust it, navigate by and absorb its Light. All of this increases our capacities, especially to love, encourage and care for others, and to help us fully trust and accept their love in return.

As we strive to do this, neither fear itself nor whatever we might be afraid of can overcome us in the long race. Never. No matter the circumstances. Just ask the voices of Leningrad, or Auschwitz—or the authors you find here, some of whom have endured their own personal holocaust and imprisoning fears.

Peter, Paul, and James know a little something firsthand about the source of this Light and Power that kindles our own flame and keeps the embers burning within, warm and glowing.

The Miracle of Love

This anthology has covered a lot of ground, including many stories from a swath of experience so humbly, willingly shared. Passages in which individuals faced a terrible fear in some cases. Some narratives speak to powerfully unselfish acts towards others who seemingly didn't deserve the clemency offered.

Other stories speak to basic survival, if not physical than psychological, emotional—spiritual. These illustrate the importance of essential healthy respect for self. They describe a basic dignity we must maintain within us to have any quality of life.

The passages of these pages show the strength needed at our core to have hope and that, in time, we will move forward. In some stories here, the fear told of speaks to survival instincts. We have also been shown that sometimes, extreme cases call for extreme courage, strength and resilience—and what that looks like for some unimaginable circumstance to be overcome.

A miracle is a shift in perception from fear to love.
Marianne Williamson

This of course, by necessity, is oft born of the healthy, balanced care of self as much as the possession of a charitable posture towards others.

Other times the answer is to venture more outside of ourselves; wherein we need to set our fears aside the best we are able and reach out to someone else. It can be ironically liberating and helpful to focus less on what we need, and more about giving all the love we can, that is needed around us.

After all, much of our own suffering enables us to intuitively understand what others need, because it is often exactly what we have needed at one time or another. Perhaps we have even experienced a sensitizing void and famish of just the same.

Some would say that our experiential understanding makes it essentially obligatory for us to reach back to others. When we find the courage to do so, we find purpose and healing. It is here we find the miracles of reciprocity. And it is here where our gratitude flourishes, overcoming all. Or as the disciple put it in Matthew 13:13:

And now abides faith, hope, love, these three;
but the greatest of these is love.

As *Intercession* speaks to—this read hopes to remind of the importance of love for and faith in others, in ourselves, and in that all-important Light far beyond our fullness of understanding. This Light, our God, is both our Origin and our Destiny. He is the essence of love, capable of creation, healing, fulfillment, and a proclivity for enlightening us.

I am referring to that which offers the best, most enduring answers to all our fears. That which we sometimes can only find as we grope our way through great, dark corridors of fear.

In the sublime words of a literary icon—at the close of a letter she wrote long ago, I leave you with this timeless salutation.

"…the real things haven't changed. It is still best to be honest and truthful; to make the most of what we have; to be happy with simple pleasures and to be cheerful and have courage when things go wrong. With love to you all and best wishes for your happiness,

I am,

Yours sincerely.
—Laura Ingalls Wilder

Poetic Pause

Poetry Pebbles

There isn't a particle of life which doesn't bear poetry in it.
Gustave Flaubert (1821–1880)

Poetry is nearer to vital truth than history.
Leonardo da Vinci

The Elderly Gentleman

By George Canning

By the side of a murmuring stream, an elderly gentleman sat.
On the top of his head was a wig, and a top of his wig was his hat.
The wind it blew high and blew strong,
As the elderly gentleman sat;
And bore from his head in a trice, and plunged in the river his hat.
The gentleman then took his cane which lay by his side as he sat;
And he dropped in the river his wig,
In attempting to get out his hat.
His breast, it grew cold with despair,
And full in his eye madness sat;
So he flung in the river his cane to swim with his wig and his hat.
Cool reflection, at last, came across
While this elderly gentleman sat;
So he thought he would follow the stream
And look for his cane, wig, and hat.
His head thicker than common, o'er-balanced the rest of his fat;
And in plumped this son of a woman
To follow his wig, cane, and hat.

NOTE: Only those who have NEVER made a simple situation worse, all on your very own - may laugh AT this poor fellow. The rest of us will laugh WITH him.

The thing in the world I am most afraid of is fear, with good reason; that passion alone, in the trouble of it, exceeds all other accidents.

Michel de Montaigne, Essays, Fear. (1850)

CHAPTER 10

For the Love Of Quotes

Inspired

Fear grid-irons your broken, suffering heart with, at least an initial sense of strength, enclosing it with a protective, tough outer-shell; this encasing eventually becomes a prison that will emaciate the unused, enclosed heart inside if left too long to its own accord.
Renewed hope gently unwraps the hard cast, and replaces it with a more resilient, pliable layer; protective, strong, but permeable so as to let love and light in and nurture the otherwise malnourished, dying heart inside.

Connie Kerbs

The greatest weakness of all weaknesses is to fear too much to appear weak.

Jacques-Bénigne Bossuet (1709)

Obstacles are like wild animals. They are cowards, but they will bluff you if they can. If they see you are afraid of them...they are liable to spring upon you; but if you look them squarely in the eye, they will slink out of sight.

Orison Swett Marden

Fear grows in darkness; If you think there's a bogeyman around, turn on the light.

Dorothy Thompson

Pebbles To Pocket: Overcoming Fear

A Collection of Novice Voices
& Sages of the Ages

Obedient to the goad of grief,
Her steps, now fast, now lingering slow,
In varying motion seek relief
From the Eumenides of woe…
Charlotte Brontë (Excerpt from "Francis," Poem)

In skating over thin ice, our safety is in our speed.
Ralph Waldo Emerson

Above all to thine own self, be true.
William Shakespeare

Painful as it may be, a significant emotional event can be the catalyst for choosing a direction that serves us—and those around us—more effectively. Look for the learning.
Louisa May Alcott

Pray tell, should we really have any more angst about death than we might for the middle act of an epic play.
Connie Kerbs

What lies behind us and what lies before us
are tiny matters compared to what lies within us.
Ralph Waldo Emerson

The thing I fear most is fear.
Michel de Montaigne, Essais, Book I, Chapter 18 (1580).

Fear is sharp-sighted, and can see things underground,
and much more in the skies.

Miguel de Cervantes (1605-1615).

I was astounded, my hair stood on end,
and my voice stuck in my throat.

Virgil, Æneid (29-19 BC), II. 774, and III. 48.

I know that oft we tremble at an empty terror, but the
false phantasm brings a real misery.

Friedrich Schiller

Withhold no sacrifice, begrudge no toil, seek no sordid gain,
fear no foe, all will be well.

Winston Churchill

Like one that on a lonesome road
Doth walk in fear and dread,
And having once turned round walks on,
And turns no more his head;
Because he knows, a frightful fiend
Doth close behind him tread.

Samuel Taylor Coleridge, The Rime of the Ancient Mariner,

When the truth cannot be clearly made out,
what is false is increased through fear.

Quintus Curtius Rufus,

We are, all of us – failures. At least, the best of us are.
James Barrie Let us never negotiate out of fear.
But let us never fear to negotiate.

John F. Kennedy, Inaugural Address (January 20, 1961)

Remember, adjusting your mindset for success is at least half the battle of
anything. In the case of overcoming our fear, it is 99% of a war
waged in our own head.

Connie Kerbs

*One of the greatest discoveries a man makes,
one of his great surprises is to find
that he can do what he was afraid he couldn't do.*
Henry Ford.

Fear is the main source of superstition, and one of the main sources of cruelty. To conquer fear is the beginning of wisdom.
Bertrand Russell

Fear always springs from ignorance.
Ralph Waldo Emerson

No passion so effectually robs the mind of all its powers of acting and reasoning as fear.
Edmund Burke

Freedom from fear...sums up the...philosophy of human rights.
Thomas Jefferson

The fear of someone else's fate of falling off where we hung precariously before being rescued, necessitates our own reaching back. We simply just must guide, support, help, and encourage others who similarly stumble. We simply must return the favor of any life-saving, soul saving or emotional life preservers which were once thrown to us.
Connie Kerbs

Find ecstasy in life; the mere sense of living is joy enough.
Emily Dickinson

Taking a new step, uttering a new word, is what people fear...
Fyodor Dostoevsky Crime and Punishment Part I, Ch. 1 (1866).

Death in itself is nothing, but we fear to be we know not what, we know not where.
John Dryden, Aureng-Zebe, Act IV, scene I (1676)

Endurance is patience concentrated.
Thomas Carlyle

Where there is charity and wisdom, there is neither fear nor ignorance.
Francis of Assisi

Out of timber so crooked as that from which man is made nothing entirely straight can be carved.

Immanuel Kant

To laugh often and much;
To win the respect of intelligent people
And the affection of children;
To earn the appreciation of honest critics
And endure the betrayal of false friends;
To appreciate beauty, to find the best in others;
To leave the world a bit better,
Whether by a healthy child, a garden patch,
Or a redeemed social condition;
To know even one life has breathed easier
Because you have lived.
This is to have succeeded.

Ralph Waldo Emerson

We are not here concerned with hopes or fears, only with truth as far as our reason permits us to discover it.

Charles Darwin, The Descent of Man

Sorrow is better than fear. Fear is a journey, a terrible journey. But, sorrow is at least an arriving.

Alan Paton

We all fear the unfamiliar, the unseen, and the unknown, at least most of us do, at least sometime. Well, if we are honest about it. It's only normal and natural.

Connie Kerbs

Love will find a way through paths where wolves fear to prey.

Lord Byron

Where fear is, happiness is not.

Lucius Annaeus Seneca

Poetic Pause

Poetry Pebbles

Learn poetry by heart. If you know a poem by heart, no one can take it away from you, and you can take advantage of it anytime.

Raymond Aubrac

Ordering a man to write a poem is like commanding a pregnant woman to give birth to a red-headed child.

Carl Sandburg

Epitaph

Samuel Taylor Coleridge

*'Stop, Christian Passer-by! - Stop, child of God,
And read with gentle breast. Beneath this sod
A poet lies, or that which once seem'd he. -
O, lift one thought in prayer for S.T.C.;
That he who many a year with toil of breath
Found death in life, may here find life in death!
Mercy for praise - to be forgiven for fame
He ask'd for praise - to be forgiven for fame
He ask'd, and hoped, through Christ.
Do thou the same!*

Samuel Taylor Coleridge (1772-1834)
After being moved from his original internment at Old Highgate Chapel,
the poet now rests at the aisle of St. Michael's Church,
Highgate, London, England.
The above was his self-written epitaph.

Samuel Taylor Coleridge was an English poet, literary critic, philosopher, and theologian. With his friend, William Wordsworth, whom he was a great influence upon, they would ultimately father the Romantic Movement in England. He is most well-known for poems, The Rime of the Ancient Mariner and Kubla Khan, as well as the major prose work Biographia Literaria. His critical work on William Shakespeare was highly influential, and he helped introduce German idealist philosophy to the English-speaking culture. Coleridge is one of the most important figures in English poetry. His poems directly and deeply influenced all the major poets of the age. He was known by his contemporaries as a meticulous craftsman who was more rigorous in his careful reworking of his poems than any other poet, and Southey and Wordsworth were dependent on his professional advice.

His influence on Wordsworth is particularly important because many critics have credited Coleridge with the very idea of "Conversational Poetry." The idea of utilizing common, everyday language to express profound poetic images and ideas for which Wordsworth became so famous, seems to have originated almost entirely with Coleridge. It is difficult to imagine Wordsworth's great poems, The Excursion or The Prelude, ever having been written without the direct influence of "STC's" originality.

Engraving by Gustave Doré for an 1876 edition of the Rime of the Ancient Mariner by Samuel Coleridge. Labeled "The Albatross." It depicts 17 sailors on the deck of a wooden ship facing an albatross. Icicles hang from the rigging.

https://commons.wikimedia.org/wiki/File:Rime_of_the_Ancient_Mariner-Albatross-Dore.jpg

"He prayeth best, who loveth best
All things both great and small;
For the dear God who loveth us;
He made and loveth all."

Samuel Taylor Coleridge
(From the Rime of the Ancient Mariner)

CHAPTER 11

Precious Pearls

Inspired

A man wrapped up in himself makes a very small bundle.
Benjamin Franklin

*Try a thing you haven't done three times.
Once, to get over the fear of doing it.
Twice, to learn how to do it.
And a third time to figure out
Whether you like it or not.*
Virgil Thomson

Above all to thine own self, be true.
William Shakespeare

To love another person is to see the face of God.
Victor Hugo

It is a press, certainly, but a press from which shall flow in inexhaustible streams...Through it, God will spread His Word. A spring of truth shall flow from it: like a new star it shall scatter the darkness of ignorance, and cause a light heretofore unknown to shine amongst men.
Johannes Gutenberg

"The Love of God."

Meir Ben Isaac Nehorai's
(The Akdumut, circa 1050)

Could we with ink the ocean fill,
And were the heavens of parchment made,
Were every stalk on earth a quill,
And every man a scribe by trade;
To write the love of God above,
Would drain the ocean dry;
Nor could the scroll contain the whole,
Though stretched from sky to sky.

From the Traditional Hymn finished by W.W. Mays, daughter of F.M. Lehman in the Early 20th Century, who wrote the melody for what was discovered mysteriously etched by an inpatient in the 19th Century, and would be finally discovered to be from the Hymnology of the Synagogue used for The Feast of Weeks (the Jewish Pentecost), which comes from works translated by Rabbi Meir ben Isaac in the 18th Century, who originally found it from Meir Ben Isaac Nehorai's Akdumut, circa 1050...among other corners of antiquity it echoes from.[1].

I love the history of this writing. The story goes that it was discovered scrawled upon a mental hospital's wall in the room of a humble, deceased patient in the 19th century. It was only found, aged and long since scribbled behind his bed, as his emptied room was being readied for the next patient.

The thought of it impressing the patient enough to etch it upon the wall suggests it provided some relief to the suffering of the poor man's lonely and humble lot in life. Perhaps he drew comfort from the idea that God had not forgotten him.

The story inspired Frederick Lehman to begin penning verses to go with it in a traditional hymn. The story and the growingly famous verse would likewise strike a chord in many believers when they heard the details. The compelling words and where they came from became a permeating testament of God's boundless love – and continued to be shared and passed on.

The story began to be retold, resonating hearts along the way. It was an oft-quoted piece of the early 20th century. Two more stanzas and chorus were added to a simple melody written by F.M. Lehman. The above became the final, climactic lines of the would-be hymn. The melody was eventually harmonized by his daughter, Mrs. W.W. Mays, and has remained well loved....but there is more.

The piece often left people with a heart-stirring ring, a haunting feeling even, that perhaps it echoed from a different place and time. People who heard the story of its assuaging the troubled man wondered if he had written it himself or found it.

After an endless search in a pre-internet world, someone happened to ask a Jewish rabbi about it, and a little light was shed! It seems that the stirring lines had touched others enough to keep bringing it forward from the distant past, this time from Rabbi Hertz, chief rabbi in the British Empire. The rabbi explained, "Go to a Jewish bookstore and on page 213 of a book entitled, *A Book on Jewish Thought* you will find this poem, translated by Rabbi Hertz, was actually written in A.D. 1050 by a Jewish poet, Meir Ben Isaac Nehorai."

In fact, it is in the hymnology of the synagogue used for the Feast of Weeks (the Jewish Pentecost). It is from the Akdamut. It also has parallels in the Koran, and many other ancient texts.

It is not difficult to imagine the original poet(s), staring up into the vast, ancient sky, heart(s)s bursting with thoughts of an omniscient, awesome Creator capable of such wonder. Interestingly, several other similar, analogous writings exist. Perhaps an older, original piece inspired the remnants we have now? Either way, its evidence that deep truths tell and re-tell themselves beautifully.

"The Love of God"

The love of God is greater far
Than tongue or pen can ever tell;
It goes beyond the highest star,
And reaches to the lowest hell;
The guilty pair, bowed down with care,
God gave His Son to win;
His erring child He reconciled,
And pardoned from his sin.

When hoary time shall pass away,
And earthly thrones and kingdoms fall,
When men who here refuse to pray,
On rocks and hills and mountains call,
God's love so sure, shall still endure,
All measureless and strong;
Redeeming grace to Adam's race —
The saints' and angels' song.

Could we with ink the ocean fill...
(See article above.)

Refrain:
Oh, love of God, how rich and pure!
How measureless and strong!
It shall forevermore endure —
The saints' and angels' song.

Frederick Lehman*

Seasons

Anonymous, from Ecclesiastes (KJV)

To everything there is a season,
And a time to every purpose under the heaven:
A time to be born, a time to die; a time to plant,
And a time to pluck up that which is planted;
A time to kill, and a time to heal;
A time to break down, and a time to build up;
A time to weep, and a time to laugh;
A time to mourn, and a time to dance;
A time to cast away stones,
And a time to gather stones together;
A time to embrace,
A time to refrain from embracing;
A time to get, and a time to lose;
A time to keep, and a time to cast away;
A time to rend, and a time to sew;
A time to keep silence, and a time to speak;
A time to love, and a time to hate;
A time of war, and a time of peace.

Ecclesiastes 3: 1-8 (KJV)

Life can only be understood backward, but it must be lived forward.
Soren Kierkegaard

Beauty for Ashes

The Prophet Isaiah (KJV)

The Spirit of the Lord, God,
Is upon me…
To appoint unto them
That mourn in Zion,
To give unto them beauty for ashes,
The oil of joy for mourning,
The garment of praise
For the spirit of heaviness;
That they might be called
Trees of righteousness,
The planting of the Lord,
That He might be glorified.

Isaiah 61: 1-3 (KJV)

For wisdom is better than jewels;
And all desirable things cannot compare with her.

Proverbs 8:11

Amazing Grace

By John Newton (1725-1807)

Amazing Grace, how sweet the sound,
That saved a wretch like me.
I once was lost but now am found,
Was blind, but now I see.

T'was Grace that taught my heart to fear.
And Grace, my fears relieved.
How precious did that Grace appear
The hour I first believed.

Through many dangers, toils, and snares
I have already come;
'Tis Grace that brought me safe thus far
And Grace will lead me home.

The Lord has promised good to me.
His word my hope secures.
He will my shield and portion be,
As long as life endures.

Yea, when this flesh and heart shall fail,
And mortal life shall cease,
I shall possess within the veil,

A life of joy and peace.

When we've been there ten thousand years
Bright shining as the sun.
We've no less days to sing God's praise
Then when we've first begun.

Amazing Grace, how sweet the sound,
That saved a wretch like me.
I once was lost but now am found,
Was blind, but now I see...

"**A**mazing Grace" is a Christian hymn published in 1779, written by English poet and clergyman, John Newton (1725–1807).

Originally conscripted into the Royal Navy, turned Atlantic slave-trader, Newton didn't begin religious or convicted. Then, in 1748, a violent storm battered his vessel off the coast of County Donegal, Ireland. In his trial, he called out to God for mercy, which ultimately marked his Christian conversion. He ended his seafaring around 1754 and began studying theology.

Ordained in the Church of England in 1764, Newton began to write hymns with poet William Cowper. "Amazing Grace" was written to illustrate a sermon on New Year's Day of 1773.

It has been associated with more than 20 melodies, but in 1835 it was joined to a tune named "New Britain" to which it is most frequently sung today.

With the message that forgiveness and redemption are possible regardless of sin, and that the soul can be delivered from despair through the mercy of God, "Amazing Grace" is one of the most recognizable songs in the English-speaking world.

Author Gilbert Chase writes it is "…the most famous of all the folk hymns…" Jonathan Aitken, Newton biographer, estimates it is performed 10 million times annually, worldwide.

*…Be filled with the spirit, speaking to one another with psalms, hymns, and songs from the Spirit.
Sing and make music from your heart to the Lord…*
Ephesians 5:18-19

In Flanders Fields

By Lieutenant-Colonel John McCrae

In Flanders fields the poppies blow
Between the crosses, row on row,
That mark our place; and in the sky
The larks, still bravely singing, fly
Scarce heard amid the guns below.

We are the Dead. Short days ago
We lived, felt dawn, saw sunset glow,
Loved and were loved, and now we lie
In Flanders fields.

Take up our quarrel with the foe:
To you from failing hands we throw
The torch; be yours to hold it high.
If ye break faith with us who die
We shall not sleep, though poppies grow
In Flanders fields.

While the original wording has been off and on disputed, this is the version as printed in *In Flanders Fields and Other Poems*, a 1919 collection of McCrae's works. For a poem, that, as the story goes, was retrieved out of the trash by comrades, and sent in for publication initially unbeknownst to its author, after McCrae, disappointed in it, had tossed it aside—it didn't do too bad.

In fact, it would go on to become one of the most successful, beloved war poems of all time, a symbol of WWI, and eventually an enduring emblem of remembrance of all wars, coupled with the bright Red Poppy whose imagery is invoked so poignantly in this touching, poignant work, now known and loved the world over.

McCrae fought in the second battle of Ypres in the Flanders region of Belgium. The German army launched one of the first chemical attacks in the history of war but was unable to break through the Canadian line, which held for over two weeks. In a letter written to his mother, McCrae described the battle as a "nightmare":

"For seventeen days and seventeen nights none of us have had our clothes off, nor even our boots, except occasionally. In all that time while I was awake, gunfire and rifle fire never ceased for sixty seconds... And behind it all was the constant background of the sights of the dead, the wounded, the maimed, and a terrible anxiety lest the line should give way."

Alexis Helmer, a close friend, was killed during the battle on May 2. McCrae performed the burial service himself, at which time he noted how poppies quickly grew around the graves of those who died at Ypres. The next day, he composed the poem while sitting in the back of an ambulance at an Advanced Dressing Station outside Ypres. This location is today known as the John McCrae Memorial Site.

"In Flanders Fields" was the most popular poem of its era. The poem was republished throughout the world, rapidly becoming synonymous with the sacrifice of the soldiers who died in the First World War. Its appeal was universal. Soldiers took encouragement from it as a statement of their duty to those who died while people on the home front viewed it as defining the cause for which their brothers and sons were fighting. (14)

The best remedy for those who are afraid, lonely or unhappy
is to go outside, somewhere where they can be quiet,
alone with the heavens, nature, and God.
Because only then does one feel that all is as it should be
and that God wishes to see people happy,
amidst the simple beauty of nature.

Ann Frank

Nothing Gold Can Stay

By Robert Lee Frost

Nature's first green is gold,
Her hardest hue to hold.
Her early leaf's a flower;
But only so an hour.
Then leaf subsides to leaf.
So Eden sank to grief,
So dawn goes down to day.
Nothing gold can stay.

"Nothing Gold Can Stay" is a poem by Robert Frost, written and published in the Yale Review in 1923. Later published in the collection, New Hampshire (1923; copyright renewed 1951), which earned Frost the 1924 Pulitzer Prize for Poetry.

Alfred R. Ferguson wrote of the poem, "Perhaps no single poem more fully embodies the ambiguous balance between paradisiac good and the paradoxically more fruitful human good than 'Nothing Gold Can Stay…'"

Many cultural references have arisen out of the work, including the 1967 novel The Outsiders by S. E. Hinton and it's 1983 film adaptation where the character Ponyboy recites it aloud. (15).

...When old age shall this generation waste,
Thou shalt remain, in midst of other woe
Than ours, a friend to man, to whom thou sayst,
"Beauty is truth, truth beauty," - that is all
Ye know on earth, and all ye need to know.

John Keats
(From the last stanza of Ode on a Grecian Urn)

More Inspirational Pebbles On Anything and Everything

Gathered by Connie Kerbs

*Do you want to know who you are? Don't ask. Act!
Action will delineate and define you.*

Thomas Jefferson

*I am simply a 'book drunkard.' Books have the same irresistible temptation for me that liquor has for its devotee.
I cannot withstand them.*

L.M. Montgomery

Obedience, Responsibility, Rules, and Safety are loyal, inseparable playmates. Love is their wise mother, who knows there are times to break them up. At least once in a while, for a bit, lest they get into some kind of arrogant, bullish, mischief. Lest they completely shut out their other siblings — Joy, Compassion, Common sense, and the one and only spoilt, youngest sibling, Exception to Every Rule.

Connie Kerbs

*I was obliged to be industrious.
Whoever is equally industrious will succeed equally well.*

Johann Sebastian Bach

I am in the land of the dying, and I am soon going to the land of the living.

John Newton (last words)

*Happiness is a butterfly, which, when pursued, is always just beyond your grasp, but which, if you will sit down quietly,
may alight upon you.*

Nathaniel Hawthorne

*For the pride of trace and trail was his, and sick unto death,
he could not bear that another dog should do his work.*

Jack London, The Call of the Wild

*Two things awe me most, the starry sky above me
and the moral law within me.*

Immanuel Kant

*There are seasons, in human affairs, of inward and outward revolution, when new depths seem to be broken up in the soul when new wants are unfolded in multitudes, and a new and undefined good is thirsted for. There are periods when...
to dare is the highest wisdom.*

Elizabeth Barrett Browning, (1860)

Find ecstasy in life; the mere sense of living is joy enough.

Emily Dickinson doesn't know what I may seem to the world. But to myself I seem to have been only a boy playing on the seashore, diverting myself in now and then finding a smoother pebble or prettier shell than ordinary, whilst the great ocean of truth lay undiscovered before me.

Isaac Newton

*Most folks are about as happy
as they make up their minds to be.*

Abraham Lincoln

*In the realm of ideas, everything depends on enthusiasm...
in the real world, all rests on perseverance.*

Johann Wolfgang von Goethe

The superior weapon of choice to fight ineffective, unwarranted distrust and fear, is a commitment to believing in the best of intent of others, coupled with a charitable heart which tolerates the differences and imperfection in each of us. It is then the struggle shifts to what it ought to be, and our intellect and reasoning can be successfully employed to deal with such negative emotions.

Connie Kerbs

Whatever you are, be a good one.

Abraham Lincoln

*In this one book are the two most interesting personalities...
God and yourself. The Bible is the story of God and man, a love story in which you and I must write our own ending, our unfinished autobiography of the creature and the Creator.*
Fulton Oursler

*I know not with what weapons World War III will be fought,
but World War IV will be fought with sticks and stones.*
Albert Einstein

There is nothing to fear except the persistent refusal to find out the truth, the persistent refusal to analyze the causes of happenings.
Dorothy Thompson

You can search throughout the entire universe for someone who is more deserving of your love and affection than you are yourself, and that person is not to be found anywhere. You, yourself, as much as anybody in the entire universe deserves your love and affection.
Buddha

Accept the things which fate binds you and love the people whom fate brings you together, but do so with all your heart.
Marcus Aurelius

*Good, Better, Best. Never let it rest.
Til your good is better and your better is best.*
St. Jerome

*Do what you love. Know your own bone —
gnaw at it, bury it, unearth it and gnaw it still.*
Henry David Thoreau

Life itself is a quotation.
Jorge Luis Borges

Poetic Pause

Poetry Pebbles

Never did Poesy appear
So full of heaven to me, as when
I saw how it would pierce through pride and fear
To the lives of coarsest men.
　　　　James Russell Lowell

Poetry is pulled out of life experience as sea-salt
is distilled out of ocean water.
　　　　Connie Kerbs

Love and Fear

By G.W. Mercure

If you could look inside a man's heart
Beyond that flush, which stops and starts,
That flesh that swells, that blood that darts,
That beat, that beat, the most human art,
To where in kind,
The boiling mind
Crashes blind
Against the grind
Of that counting claret core and finds
All rage, all gentles entwined,
All passion, all tenderness assigned,
From but two sources only mined:
If you could look inside a man's heart
All there is there to find
Are love and fear.

G.W. Mercure is a writer from Providence, Rhode Island. He wishes only to leave readers with this quote: "The world doesn't need to find more writers; the world needs more teachers."

There are two ways of spreading light:
to be the candle or the mirror that reflects it.
Edith Wharton

CHAPTER 12

Pondering Poetry

Inspired

To Lord Byron
By John Keats

Byron! How sweetly sad thy melody!
Attuning still the soul to tenderness,
As if soft Pity, with unusual stress,
Had touch'd her plaintive lute, and thou, being by,
Hadst caught the tones, nor suffer'd them to die.
O'ershadowing sorrow doth not make thee less
Delightful: thou thy griefs dost dress
With a bright halo, shining beamily,
As when a cloud the golden moon doth veil,
Its sides are ting'd with a resplendent glow,
Through the dark robe oft amber rays prevail,
And like fair veins in sable marble flow;
Still warble, dying swan! still tell the tale,
The enchanting tale, the tale of pleasing woe.

Lord Houghton in Life, John Keats is a dominant poet of the English Romantic era. His works were only published (and only reluctantly received) for a few years before his early death in 1821, at the age of 25. His posthumous fame would rise unprecedentedly. He remains one of the most beloved poets of all time, and his body of work casts a wide net of influence. (16).

Some Prosy on Poesy

By Connie Kerbs

Poetry can seem mysterious, even strange. But, like the salt of the sea or a clam's precious pearl - poetry is the kernel of experience. Living and life are the inspiration from which all great poetry flows. Although not entirely necessary for some uber talented poets, and even less necessary to enjoy reading poetry, it helps tremendously to know something about meter, rhyme, tempo, and form. In writing poetry, it helps, even more, to be open to criticism, and have a mindset prepared to work a poem, edit and re-edit, shape it and re-shape it, again and again.

Successful poets also remember there is a time to accept where it is at and move on because there is no such thing as a perfect or even finished poem.

And then there is this: some poems flow easily, right out of the heart's gate. Others take decades to finish themselves. After all, a poet doesn't *really* write the poem – the poem tells itself. It is the verse of creativity and life. The poet is a conduit, a pen holder, a transcriber of the intangible, creative subconscious.

Poetry is simply a testimony of what the poet has felt, seen, and heard. It is a parable of learning to love a piece of life, exploring what it means to us, contemplating how it has changed us – and then learning to let go of it.

Poetry, itself is a witty, highly efficient metaphor; a delightful ditty which describes how life changes, challenges or charms us in some way.

Ye stars! Which are the poetry of heaven!
Lord Byron

More Pebbles On Poetry

Collected by Connie Kerbs

Beauty of whatever kind, in its supreme development, invariably excites the sensitive soul to tears.
Edgar Allan Poe

Poetry is when an emotion has found its thought, and the thought has found words.
Robert Frost

Poetry is thoughts that breathe, and words that burn.
Thomas Gray

I was reading the dictionary. I thought it was a poem about everything.
Steven Wright

Poetry is a deal of joy and pain and wonder, with a dash of the dictionary.
Kahlil Gibran

The crown of literature is poetry.
W. Somerset Maugham

Teach your children poetry; it opens the mind, lends grace to wisdom and makes the heroic virtues hereditary.
Walter Scott

Poetry is the journal of a sea animal living on land, wanting to fly in the air.
Carl Sandburg

God is the perfect poet.
Robert Browning

The poet is only the conduit, a transcriber,
for a most truthful testimony of a life fully lived.
Connie Kerbs

Poetry is the essence of reckless abandonment. It is also a channel for things needing to be expressed that could otherwise never be — things which have oft waited far too long for dignity and the light of day. It is a canal leading to the light of an opening, for those buried, dark and self-censored things, the ones banished even from our thoughts.
Connie Kerbs

My life has been the poem I would have writ,
But I could not both live and utter it.
Henry David Thoreau

Publishing a volume of verse is like dropping a rose petal
down the Grand Canyon and waiting for the echo.
Don Marquis

A great poet is the most precious jewel of a nation.
Ludwig van Beethoven

Universal truths are transparent and obvious. These bold ideas wax poetic and beautiful, often over great arches of time and place.
These blatant truths flourish through story, art, and epic poetry.
Connie Kerbs

It is absurd to think that the only way to tell if a poem is lasting is to wait and see if it lasts. The right reader of a good poem can tell the moment it strikes him that he has taken an immortal wound — that he will never get over it.
Robert Frost

Poetic Pause

Poetry Pebbles

A poem begins in delight and ends in wisdom.
　　　　　　　　　Robert Frost

Poetry is the revelation of a feeling that the poet believes to be interior and personal which the reader recognizes as his own.
　　　　　　　Salvatore Quasimodo

Poetry's Space

By Connie Kerbs

Part 1 from Poetry's Palace
Poetry's space preserves the silent sounds
Of a billion, basking, breathing features
On a puzzled globe, outlined with
Sanded, rocky, living, busy beaches.
Life, anonymous, teems in tide pools,
Layers of creatures yearn for the return
Of the tide's quenching, caressing foam
Ebbing and flowing mysterious reaches.

Poetry's space pauses time imperceptible
Between flutters of hummingbird wings
Flitting, lively, vivid, pointy passengers
Ever piercing, probing for succulent nectar.
And poetry's heart throbs warm and deep
With fierce and ferocious motherly love
For any tender offspring dependent on`
A determined, devoted parental protector.

Poetry's space is an oversized Harvest Moon
Hovering on the horizon, jaw-dropping low.
The sunset it captured and trapped inside
Burns brilliant; with a bright, blood-orange glow.
Its mysterious, marbled; illumination,
And marvelous, mottled presentation spurs our curiosity.
It inspires our imagination's astral aspirations.
Captivating! Fascinating! Deserving of telescopic appreciation and
Studious observation. A superb ovation for such a stellar show.

Poetry's space is a dense thicket of countless, invisible crickets
Ever cheeping and chirping their charming, chipper melody.
Its' a wild, winsome song that winds up the woods all night long.
It's a superb orchestra of miniature organic, translucent bows;
Proud, loud, dusk till dawn, it's a curiously conspicuous chorus.
A zany, crazy, chorale society that sings with its wings, so amorous.
It's a distinct, instinctive encore of talented courtiers out to woo.
True, such an orgy in certain circles would certainly be taboo.
But in this poetic space, its impressive, these expressive little beaus.

Poetry .is the expression of our wonder and marveling over something observed or felt.

Connie Kerbs.

CHAPTER 13

The Beginning Of the End

Inspired

I am convinced with Plato,
With St. Paul, with St. Augustine,
With Calvin, and with Leibnitz,
That this universe, and every
Smallest portion of it exactly fulfills
The purpose for which almighty God
Designed it.

James Anthony Froude

Word

Martin Luther

The Unchanging Word

Feelings come and feelings go,
And feelings are deceiving;
My warrant is the Word of God—
Naught else is worth believing.

Though all my heart should feel condemned
For want of some sweet token,
There is One greater than my heart
Whose Word cannot be broken.

I'll trust in God's unchanging Word
Till soul and body sever,
For, though all things shall pass away,
HIS WORD SHALL STAND FOREVER!

Therefore, whosoever heareth these sayings of mine, and doeth them, I will liken him unto a wise man, which built his house upon a rock.

Matthew 7:24

An Intercession

By Paul, the Apostle

I leave you now with an excerpt from the Apostle Paul's words from a passage that has been described by some biblical scholars as some of the purest text of the New Testament: the Apostle's "magnum opus." The Epistle to the Romans offers insight into the Christian faith as understood and defined by Paul. This passage, from the last section in Romans 8 is a most personal and eloquent testimony, one which resonates so deeply with my own:

Likewise, the Spirit also helpeth our infirmities:
For we know not what we should pray for
As we ought:
But the Spirit itself maketh intercession for us
With groanings which cannot be uttered...
For I am persuaded, that neither death nor life,
Nor angels, nor principalities, nor powers,
Nor things present, nor things to come;
Nor height, nor depth, nor any other creature
Shall be able to separate us from the love of God
Which is in Christ Jesus our Lord.

Romans 8: 26 & 38-39

The LORD, thy God
In the midst of thee, is mighty;
He will save,
He will rejoice over thee with joy;
He will rest in his love,
He will joy over thee with singing.

Zephaniah 3:17

Bibliography

1. Wikiquote (2016, July 15) God. July 21
   https://en.wikiquote.org/w/index.php?title=God&oldid=226968

2. Williamson, Marianne. A Return to Love: Reflections on the Principles of A Course in Miracles. New York: HarperPerennial, 2012. Print.

3. Wikisource. 2015, Dec 27) Work, Love, and Life, 29 Dec 2015.https://en.wikisource.org/wiki/Three_Best_Things

4. Wikipedia (2016, Jan 11) Henry van Dyke, Jr. 12 Jan 2016

5. Wikisource (2015, Dec 27) The Sick Child, 28 Dec 2015.
   https://en.wikisource.org/wiki/Underwoods/The_Sick_Child

6. WikiSource (2015, Dec 27) Robert Louis Stevenson, (29 Dec.2015).
   https://en.wikipedia.org/wiki/Robert_Louis_Stevenson

7. Wikipedia, (2015, April 3) Flight-or-Fight Response. Retrieved April 5, 2015.
   https://en.wikipedia.org/w/index.php?title=Fight-or-flight_response&oldid=796132800

8. Ingraham, Christopherson; (2014, October 30). America's Top Fears: Public Speaking, heights, and bugs. Retrieved from:
   https://www.washingtnpost.com/news/wonk/wp/2014/10/30/clowns-are-twice-as-scary-to-democrats-as-they-are-to-republicans/

9. Spenser And The Tradition. ENGLISH POETRY 1579-1830: A Night-Piece on Death. Retrieved February 12, 2016, from: http://spenserians.cath.vt.edu/TextRecord.php?textsid=33881

10. Wikipedia. (2016, January 29). Appointment in Samarra. Retrieved January 30, 2016, from: https://en.wikipedia.org/w/index.php?title=Appointment_in_Samarra&action=history

11. Wikipedia (2015, August 15). The Poets of the Tomb. Retrieved February 12, 2016, from: https://en.wikipedia.org/wiki/The_Poets_of_the_Tomb

12. Wikipedia (2015, Nov 17) Rudyard Kipling, 19 December, 2015. https://en.wikipedia.org/wiki/Rudyard_Kipling

13. Wikipedia (2015, December 3) Desiderata, 4 January, 2016. https://en.wikipedia.org/wiki/Deside rata

14. Wikipedia (2016, September 20). In Flanders Fields. September 21, 2016.From: https://en.wikipedia.org/w/index.php?title=In_Flanders_Fields&oldid=742663611

15. Wikipedia (2016, September 15). Nothing Gold Can Stay Poem. September 21, 2016. https://en.wikipedia.org/w/index.php?title=Nothing_Gold_Can_Stay_(poem)&oldid=770632995

16. Wikisource. (2016, March 21). To Lord Byron, 11 July 2016. https://en.wikisource.org/wiki/To_Lord_Byron

17. Wikisource. 2016, May 20). Archibald Macleish, 23 March 2016. https://en.wikipedia.org/w/index.php?title=Archibald_MacLeish&oldid=781318788

Note: All other quotes, poetry or other other references used in this book, not specifically cited, were either privately permissioned/licensed for use in this work or inspired by the following for more research of original ownership, publication, copywrite status, and their determined, allowable use, per fair use, or other mechanisms of open/public domain:

Wikiquote (2015, May 15) Fear. 17 May 2015.
https://en.wikiquote.org/wiki/Fear

Wikiquote (2015, July 29) Poets. 1 August 2015.
https://en.wikiquote.org/wiki/Poets

About the Author

Connie Kerbs

On having a grandmother who early encouraged me to peruse her upstairs library: this was a glorious haven, chalked full of vintage music, historical collections, and a rich selection of children's and grown-up literature. It was here I *met* most of the Caldecott and Newbery books, enduring poets, composers, story-telling icons, and countless literary giants. Indeed, I was irrevocably influenced and impressed.

On having an antique, *script*, manual typewriter tossed my way: it was an early, defining opportunity. This rhythmic machine called to me in no uncertain terms. Indeed, it nurtured my budding writer.

On being married to my childhood sweetheart and best friend for 30 years: I am indescribably grateful for our incredible journey together. We have been honed and humbled even as we've been bathed in bliss. Indeed, words fail to convey such a divine devotion.

On being adoptive-foster parents for a quarter of a century: this means bevies of babies and bus-loads of youth of all ages and backgrounds have graced our home, profoundly altering our world. With 13 adopted, and three procured conventionally, we are owned by, and answer to no less than sixteen of the most superb souls.

On my family, friends, love story, my Walk of Faith, ALL the kids over all these years, and – my writing journey: these have all made for the savoriest of lives and the ultimate "beautiful mess." Indeed, this is a term I often and accurately use to describe such a crazy-wonderful menagerie as this, which, to my great surprise and delight, has somehow chosen me! (conniekerbs.com).

About Pebbled Lane Books

"Every journey of a thousand miles begins with one small step..."
Ancient Proverb

The narratives and verses selected for the Pebbled Lane Books Series are like the pocket full of pebbles we've each curiously eyed and randomly plucked from a path or a beach littered with them, the world over. They are intriguing little stones each with their own unique characteristics and complex backstory.

Pebble lovers will appreciate the variety, the "stuff of life," that Pebbled Lane Books are made of. Poetry, quotes, and stories are clustered into universal themes for the series of titles. These clusters or *pebbles,* strive to be thoughtful, enlightening, and entertaining.

Pebbled Lane Books complements the mission of its publisher, F.I.N.E. Reads Press, offering engaging, thematic works that are encouraging and uplifting. The collection offers hearty literary experiences, which are all part of an enduring body of work.

The Pebbled Lane Books Series is an enriching discovery of perspectives. It is a nurturing of our inner-self, and boon to our understanding of things outseide of us. It is a collection to bolster personal and powerful determinations, all while offering pleasant distractions that inspire higher thinking as much as they engage our heart and soul.

Finally, in harmony with this imprint and publisher, yours truly wholeheartedly embraces and aspires to the sublime counsel of St. Paul. Here specifically, I refer to the following passage of beautiful words of faith and devotion with which he garnished our world:

Whatsoever things are true,
Whatsoever things are honest,
Whatsoever things are just,
Whatsoever things are pure;
Whatsoever things are lovely,
Whatsoever things are of good report;
If there be any virtue,
And if there be any praise;
Think on these things....

From the Book of Philemon

Pebbled Lane Books
By Connie Kerbs

For every ailment under the sun
There is a remedy, or there is none;
If there be one, try to find it;
If there be none, never mind it.

Mother Goose, 1695

Made in the USA
San Bernardino, CA
21 May 2019